SEVERE TURBULENCE

Braving the Storms, Hearing God's Voice, and Discovering Our Purpose

MATT AND DIANE ALLEN

tiny wonder
PUBLISHING

Copyright © 2024 by Matt and Diane Allen

All rights reserved. No part of this book may be used or reproduced in any manner whatsoever without written permission except in the case of brief quotations embodied in critical articles and reviews.

First published in the United States by Tiny Wonder Publishing
First Printing, 2024

ISBN: 978-1-7361181-7-7 Paperback
Library of Congress Control Number: 2024922684

Cover and Interior Design: Milan Klusacek

This book is for our beautiful daughters, Bella, Jewel, and Eden. May you realize how loved you are and embrace all that God has for you.

Love, Mom & Dad

↘ Contents

Preface by Matt Allen — 8

PART 1: THE RUNWAY

1. Flight QR708 DC to Doha — 12
2. The American Dream — 16
3. The Making of a Logo — 22
4. Big Dreams, Small Beginnings — 28
5. You're Fired — 34

PART 2: TAKEOFF

6. Kiosk Days — 44
7. Growing Pains — 52
8. The Store Opens — 58
9. Dreams & Visions — 64
10. A Home for 12 Angels — 70

PART 3: UNEXPECTED TURBULENCE

11. An Upside-Down Kingdom — 84
12. West Coast Move — 92
13. Pop-up Flop — 100
14. Crash Course in Screen Printing — 108
15. You Want to Fight?! — 114

PART 4: RESUMING THE CLIMB

16.	Angels Are Real	**124**
17.	Gold Dust & Soaring Sales	**130**
18.	When God Closes One Store...	**140**
19.	Rent Your Home Out	**148**
20.	Taking It to The Streets	**156**

PART 5: CRUISING ALTITUDE

21.	Hawaiian State of Mind	**168**
22.	Numbers Don't Lie	**176**

CLOSING

Our Prayer for You	**180**
NHiM Through the Years...	**182**
Acknowledgments	**198**
About the Authors	**204**
Connect with Us	**205**

Preface

If I were to ask you why you are alive for this very moment in history, could you tell me? At some point in life, I think everyone faces their own existential crisis. The moment when you think, "What is it all for? Why am I here?"

One day, I was talking with an Uber driver whose full-time job was nursing for the elderly. I assumed that caring for and learning from those who had lived a long life must be an enriching career. "Do you love it?" I asked. Surprisingly, he answered no. He shared how hard it was to watch people at the end of their lives, with regret weighing heavy on their hearts. Some regretted not spending enough time with loved ones. Others regretted wasting too much time on the wrong pursuits. But more than anything, most of them regretted not pursuing their purpose in life.

As a 35-year-old successful executive with a beautiful family of my own, I found myself questioning what my purpose was — and unable to answer. I was in the thick of climbing the corporate ladder, but something was nagging within me, ebbing away at my soul like a gentle whisper from God. I couldn't ignore it. My purpose was missing.

In the process of discovery, my wife Diane and I decided to take the flight of our lives — an adventure with God to follow the better path, a divine "flight plan." Over the pages of this book, we navigate the highs and the lows of this pursuit, creating a successful Christian clothing brand and relentlessly following God's voice. At times we heard His voice loud and clear. Other times we failed to hear Him clearly, and sometimes He seemed to be silent. But we've come through to the other side changed, and we know there's power in sharing the many testimonies from our journey.

We hope and pray that God brings revelation and hope to you as you read through our story. Your purpose is not elusive; it's attainable. The question "What is my purpose?" should lead us all to search beyond ourselves, and ultimately to look up.

Matt Allen, NHiM Founder

Part One

THE
RUNWAY

✈ Chapter 1

FLIGHT QR708
DC TO DOHA

DECEMBER 5, 2016

SEVERE TURBULENCE

Somewhere in the mid-Atlantic Ocean, about five hours into our flight to India from Washington D.C., the bottom of our plane dropped out. At least, that's what it felt like. I jolted awake and grabbed my husband Matt's hand as our plane dropped steeply in altitude. The sudden turbulence threw passengers from their seats. The lady who had been sitting in front of us was now sprawled on the floor in the aisle, moaning in pain. A 3-year-old boy flew out of his seat and landed in the lap of another passenger. An older woman bled from a deep cut on the crown of her head where she'd hit the ceiling. Across the way, a man yelled out in pain as he began to suffer the early stages of a heart attack.

This is not fiction, and this is no exaggeration. There were injuries, broken bones and fractures, blood and total disorientation. It was truly the scene out of a terrifying movie that no one signed up for. Screams filled the cabin and the oxygen masks deployed. The plane bounced, shook, and swayed for at least seven minutes. I'd never been in such a traumatizing situation, and seeing the fear of everyone around me made it even more stressful.

And then the worst happened. *The plane dropped again, and then again.* It was the most horrific experience of my life—and it wasn't over yet.

The man next to me hurriedly told me where to find the personal flotation device under our seats. That was *not* what I needed to hear. I tried to remain full of faith, but at that moment all I could picture was our three little girls. I pictured eight-year-old Bella, our oldest, with her shiny, long brown hair, always full of confidence. I imagined sweet Jewel, only six years old at the time, begging me at bedtime for "just one more story" with pleading, big blue eyes. And little Eden, only three yet full of personality and such a good snuggler. "God, you wouldn't, would you?" I thought to myself. The thought of them losing their parents and us never seeing them grow up was too much to handle. And talk about irony in the worst way! Here we were, headed to open an orphanage in India, yet our own children could become orphans.

All we could do was pray. Matt and I gripped each other's hands and began praying aloud as the plane plummeted and rocked uncontrollably, calling God's mighty angels to steady the plane and bring us safely to our destination. Our thoughts and hearts raced. Was this the end? Most of the passengers around us were shouting to Allah or to one of the many Hindu gods. I knew that the God we serve, the only God of this universe, was mighty enough to stop the winds and calm the storm, so I held onto hope.

God had been leading us on an extraordinary journey over the last two years. He'd shown us that we needed to hold onto faith through turbulence, looking to Him when the flight path was rough and the destination unknown. Surely He'd hear our prayers now.

God, please…

 **Chapter 2**

THE AMERICAN DREAM

2 YEARS EARLIER — MAY 2014

"Shoot for the stars, but if you happen to miss, shoot for the moon instead."

—Neil Armstrong

SEVERE TURBULENCE

Imagine a picture-perfect home, a great marriage, a successful career on an upward trajectory, three healthy kids, and extra money in the bank. Sounds like the American dream, right? In 2014, that's where my husband Matt and I found ourselves. We were pretty content—or at least it seemed so on the surface.

Matt had climbed the corporate ladder for the past 14 years at the medical manufacturer he worked for and was very successful for 35 years young. I was thriving as a stay-at-home mom of three little girls aged six, four, and one, and serving part-time as a worship leader at our local growing start-up church. I was finding newfound joy in the kitchen and used every kids' naptime as an opportunity to *pin* new recipes for family dinners. I also discovered a healthy love of running and had just completed a half-marathon. We were living in our dream home—a beautiful house in Castle Rock, Colorado—with more square footage than anyone needed, complete with an eye-catching spiral staircase and a *man-cave* garage for Matt, where he stored the Jeep from his wish-list, off-road toys, and much more.

Yet for Matt, life didn't feel so perfect. Something was missing. He felt *off* and it was starting to become more evident with his less-than-chipper-self. One night, we were walking up the spiral staircase to check on the kids to be sure they actually went to sleep after the last goodnight kiss. (They'd been known to get out of bed or to sneak into their toy drawer for a late night "playtime party.") Seeing that all was going smoothly with bedtime as our daughters were fast asleep, Matt stopped me on the way back down the stairs.

"Is this all that life is?" he asked. I was taken aback and confused. Honestly, his question bothered me. How could he think this wasn't good enough? Just look at our life! What more could we ask for? We had a beautiful family, loved each other, loved God, had great friends, and had plenty of provision.

"What do you mean?" I asked, puzzled. Matt processed things aloud for a bit before coming to the conclusion that he wanted more, but didn't know what "more" was. He felt guilty admitting that and for not being happier with how our life together was unfolding.

"It's not that I'm not thankful for you or for our family and all that God has blessed us with," he said. "I just feel empty and lost. Like I'm only working to bring home a paycheck." He explained that he felt stuck in a job that might be a dream for others but instead seemed to pull him away from the purpose he was trying to discover. The contribution or impact he wanted to make in the world wasn't there. There had to be more to life.

I tried to listen well and truly understand. Although he was helping contribute to our local church, community, and doing his best to love our neighbors, there were 8-10 hours of every day where his work felt mediocre and unfulfilling. And at the end of our lives he didn't want to look back and feel like he *missed* it, or didn't take the path God wanted him on. The career path he was on had definitely been a blessing in helping us establish our family and providing for our needs, but the mundane day-in and day-out tasks were waning on him. He had to do something with his life that made a difference.

We both knew the answer wouldn't be found in making a rash decision, so I encouraged him to turn to the Word of God to discover what he was searching for. To pray and ask God for wisdom. We went to bed and let the conversation rest. Over the coming days and weeks, we continued to pray and search the Bible for answers.

Matt felt drawn to focus on the book of Acts—a book which is so vital to us as believers. The disciples and followers of Jesus demonstrated how to *walk out* their faith under the power and influence of the Holy Spirit. Real men and women stepped out boldly for the name of Jesus and spread the gospel to different cities, people groups, and nations. The hand of God was upon their lives, allowing them to perform miracles, signs, and wonders.

As Matt revisited the book of Acts, he became increasingly intrigued by the life of Paul. In chapter 17, Paul is living in Athens, which was the *metropolis* to live in during that time in history. It was a crowded, popular city, filled with affluent and highly educated people, Greek intellectuals, philosophers, and more idols and gods than people. Paul regularly conversed and debated philosophy with the locals in the marketplaces and

SEVERE TURBULENCE

synagogues. And he knew his stuff. He was well-versed in many of the different religions, philosophies, and gods these Greeks worshiped. He often used this knowledge daily as a springboard into a mission-minded conversation about how their gods differed from the One true God.

In Acts 17:22-31, Paul gives his famous speech on Mars Hill. He tells the Athenians that he recognizes the fact that they're very religious people, as their idols and shrines are strewn throughout the city. But one of the altars is nameless, dedicated "to the unknown God." Paul uses this idol as an opportunity to show them they've been worshiping a God they don't even know. He explains that this God is the God of the heavens and of the earth and doesn't live in a building made by man, but rather is everywhere, all around us, giving life and breath to all. This God is not *unreachable*—He desires for every person to find Him and to know Him. Paul then quotes a well-known poet, using the line "for in Him we live and move and have our being." (Acts 17:28, NIV)

Matt couldn't contain his excitement. He kept sharing with me about what he was learning. That verse, Acts 17:28, gripped Matt to the core. "**IN HIM** we live and move and have our being…" It was so profound and the very core of our faith as believers. Discussing this together was revelatory. It was as if the words were jumping off the pages. We realized that we ourselves were living in a city and neighborhood not that different from Athens. From the neighbor to our right to the neighbor to our left, our street was lined with highly educated, affluent individuals possessing lots of nice "stuff."

I even saw it in the young moms I was friends with. I loved the playdates where I met new moms and helped my kids develop friendships, but some of the conversations at these get-togethers felt shallow and empty. As the kids played in the grass, we'd discuss things like the latest renovations and upgrades of our homes (which were already beautiful to begin with), or the many activities our toddlers were attending, or how to secure a spot in that popular preschool program you had to sign up for the minute your child left the hospital. Many times we showcased our favorite new products from the latest multi-level marketing business (which we were basically selling to just each other, making it difficult to determine "friend" or "customer" status).

Okay, that description might be a bit extreme, but that's how superficial the swirl of conversations felt at times. Were we putting our focus and mindset on things that really mattered? It felt like a *low-key competition* of sorts, to show who had it all together, who was the best mom, or who was most successful as a family. At the core of it all was idolatry.

Just to be clear, this isn't a shaming moment. Everyone has their own convictions on their journeys in life and with the Lord. You may wonder, "How is it idolatry to want the best for my kid? Or to want security in my finances or my job?" Those things in and of themselves are not idols, but when our success or possessions become the primary focus – coming before God – that's when idolatry forms.

And Matt and I were no exception to the rule. We'd unknowingly surrounded ourselves with plenty of idols. We went to church weekly, loved Jesus and served Him, but without the security of the "castle" we'd built around us, what would we have at the end of the day? Our life's focus needed to switch gears to be all about Jesus. And we wanted to help remind others to do the same.

The verse Matt had discovered in Acts just wouldn't leave us. The phrase "in Him" felt like a statement that held so much girth. The entirety of our lives needed to be lived "in Him." From the moment we woke, to the moment we laid our heads on our pillows, our eyes and our thoughts should be fixed on Him. And what we decided to do with our lives should be done from abiding "in Him." This phrase is all throughout the Bible.

Matt realized he wanted to create something to share with the world around this statement from Acts – a logo that could identify a person's purpose in Christ. He was tired of his work lacking significance. It was just a matter of time before he put the pieces together to form a whole new personal mission. One that we'd flesh out and embrace together. A mission that would completely change our lives and put us on a new trajectory more thrilling and daring than we ever could have dreamed.

 Chapter 3

THE MAKING OF A LOGO

"Your brand is the single most important investment you can make in your business."

—Steve Forbes

SEVERE TURBULENCE

Matt and I began dismantling our previous understanding of the American Dream in exchange for pursuing a life lived fully in Him. What would our life's work become? Could we create a logo from this biblical principle of living in Him? We kept coming back to the Apostle Paul. What Paul was living out and demonstrating in the book of Acts was fascinating. To think that he combined work and the gospel in a way that seemed so effortless and natural was compelling, to say the least. However, we know for a fact that it wasn't effortless, as he ended up sacrificing everything for the sake of the gospel, including his life. 2 Corinthians 11:25 tells us Paul was beaten with rods three times, stoned, shipwrecked, and so much more.

Paul was a skilled craftsman and also an entrepreneur in tent-making. He formed a business with ministry partners Priscilla and Aquila, yet was a die-hard messenger of the Gospel. He was able to instinctively weave the two together. This moved us to think outside the norm. We wanted to combine business with the gospel. If the logo could be crafted well, then it could be used on clothing. Clothing with the logo could be a precursor to share the hope of the gospel, or to give Christians something to resonate with when they saw or wore the logo.

We began with the words 'IN HIM' which became 'NHiM'. It was a four-letter abbreviation symbolic of living in Christ. It could be worn like a badge – something that would bring identity. The words "in Him," "in Christ," or "in the Lord" are used 164 times in the writings of Paul in the New Testament alone. For example, John 3:16 says, "For God so loved the world that he gave his one and only Son, that whoever believes in Him shall not perish but have eternal life." (New International Version) The phrase "in Him" is quintessential to living a Christian life. Anything outside of this is the antithesis of following Christ.

The research stage had begun. We studied everything out there, looking for inspiration on what our logo and hopeful clothing brand could become. We started drawing up our own version of a logo (which was pretty sad-looking, since we're not gifted at sketching). We saved photos of logos we liked and brands that we aspired to look like when it comes to style. We went to malls and Christian bookstores

THE MAKING OF A LOGO

and scoured online to get an idea of how we could be different and unique, yet still relevant.

Our original inspiration was surf and skate brands that had aesthetically pleasing logos. We talked to my brother, Mike, an amazing graphic designer who had done work for Disney, Amazon, and New Balance, and asked him to help us work out the concept. In 2014, there were only a couple Christian brands that were starting to emerge and do something outside the box from the stereotypical Christian bookstore tees. Most Christian tees were just a pun or play off a well-known logo, such as using "Jesus" in place of "Reese's." No, this needed to look much different. We wanted this to be a brand that was on trend and meaningful enough to be part of your everyday wardrobe.

We went through at least 30 concepts with Mike, narrowing it down to three logos that we thought had "wings." At this point, we were just looking at an art board to conceptualize and imagine what these logos would look like on a product. We printed them out at various sizes and actually taped them onto t-shirts and hats. (Funny, maybe, but you gotta do what you gotta do!) Back then, there weren't many websites that could simulate t-shirt designs for you, so we had to visualize it in other ways.

We narrowed our choices down to two logos: one that said "HIM" and had a nail for the "i" representing how Jesus was nailed to the cross, or an abbreviated logo that was very modern-minimalist. The 'NHiM' abbreviated logo had a lowercase "i" to represent God first. We asked around to gather the opinions of friends and family. Most everyone loved the look of the modern-minimalist 'NHiM' logo, so we went with it. Plus, some of the most timeless logos are four-letter acronyms or abbreviations that are easy to remember. Brands such as IKEA, Lego, VISA, Puma, NASA, Sony, Ford, and Jeep are all made up of just four letters.

As the saying goes, "branding is everything." Your logo and branding is the first impression your business gives. A good logo creates wonder and intrigue, giving you greater opportunity to make a lasting impression with what you offer. If the impression is strong enough, it's capable of shifting culture with a simple, singular identity that people can relate to their own lives. Iconic brands with strong logos are easily recognizable and create a sense of belonging. Industry leaders like Nike, Apple, Tesla, Disney, and Starbucks show how your connection with a brand can become part of your DNA.

Next, we had to see the NHiM brand in real-life form. We found a local screen printer and commissioned them to print just 12 shirts with the logo, 10" wide, center chest. Mike told us from experience that it's good to establish a logo in black and white. If a logo can catch on without color, it probably has potential to have lasting impact. So we printed the logo in black ink to see how it would look. At the time, soft, blended fabric shirts were really in, so we chose to print our first sample run on a gray tri-blend tee. It certainly wasn't cheap or cost-effective, but being a quality brand was important to us.

Matt left work during his lunch break to race down to the printer in Denver and meet me in the parking lot. The day we picked up the sample tees at the Denver screen printer felt monumental. This was the birthplace of a dream. To do something with purpose beyond a paycheck. Matt took one of the tees from the folded stack and tried it on before we even left the parking lot. He was smiling like a little kid on Christmas morning. It looked so official seeing the logo on a shirt! That week we gave the rest of the tees away to friends and family members and asked for feedback.

The response was encouraging. People wanted to know what "NHiM" meant. It was a springboard to talk about their mutual faith in Christ and an opportunity to share the gospel. The logo was doing exactly what we hoped for: it was a magnet. People liked it. It was a new way to bring identity to a world needing Christ. They wanted to know where they could buy one, but these were just the sample tees. We knew this could be the genesis to what we'd been searching for. The NHiM logo was born.

Now the challenge was to turn a logo into a brand that could become a lifestyle.

Evolution of the Logo

2014 NHiM

2016 **NHIM**

2020

2022

2023

2024

2024+

 **Chapter 4**

BIG DREAMS, SMALL BEGINNINGS

"Let everyone else call your idea crazy… just keep going. Don't stop. Don't even think about stopping until you get there, and don't give much thought to where 'there' is. Whatever comes, just don't stop."

—Phil Knight, from "Shoe Dog"

SEVERE TURBULENCE

Every big dream seems impossible until you do it. Could the NHiM logo become a brand that would change the standard of Christian apparel? The likelihood of a business concept working is slim. 90% of all business startups fail. That's an incredibly sobering realization. Nine out of 10 times, someone's big dream or idea just doesn't work out. But that's not a reason to give up or never start.

As our excitement built, we imagined NHiM becoming something known all around Colorado, maybe even nationwide someday. We could picture it being sold across America as the Christian "it brand." We didn't yet know if it could ever become a reality, but we had to try.

Matt and I tend to be the "all in" type. We don't just kind of do something; we go all in or do nothing at all. Our desire is to do everything with excellence. Matt has always had a great tenacity to work at something until it's "right" or the best it can be. I used to be okay with "good enough" and am super thankful that Matt has taught me to push past my comfort zone. That's the beauty of having a business partner – especially your spouse. You can lean on each other in your strengths and weaknesses. If one person needs an extra push, the other is there to do that. Or if someone needs to have a more relaxed perspective, you can gently remind them.

The First Collection

We started designing our first "drop" (aka, clothing collection). We wanted to offer garments for both men and women, in varying colors and designs with the logo. We would sit and talk for hours, sketching basic concepts and coming up with ideas of what styles and colors people would want to wear and what to convey to our designer. It felt ambitious at the time, but we created six design concepts for guys and six for girls. In music terminology, we wanted to drop a full "album," not just a "single." The collection included either the center-chest logo, the logo within a design, or the slogan "Live Move Exist NHiM," which was paraphrased from our founding verse, Acts 17:28.

After about a month of reviewing endless options of shirt colors, ink colors, placements, sizing, and pricing, we sent the tech pack to the screen printer. This time around, instead of just 12 tees, we printed a quantity of 24 for each of the 12 styles. Less than 300 shirts total is hardly anything, but for us it was a real investment in our future. It was still unproven, but it would allow us to test our concept. This time, picking up the custom clothing from the printer made the reality of the dream set in, yet we still knew it was only the starting point, with many more things to figure out.

We did our homework, studying other respectable clothing brands. In order to be taken seriously, everything mattered: from design, to product, to presentation, to marketing, to where and how to sell. All of it was vital. Converting a logo into a clothing brand takes time, determination, and will. It would be essential to have a website in order to launch, and therefore we needed to research the best available platforms to set everything up without becoming a website developer. Custom hang tags on the clothing was another "must" for us, which our designer created with our logo, website, and slogan. It was also important to convey the mission and vision behind the brand, so we made a promotional card to clearly endorse this message with style.

Since these would be sold online and at events, the product wouldn't be on a hanger, but instead folded. We learned how to fold shirts to optimally display the design, and took it a step further by inserting them in a sealed clear poly-bag. We got busy folding, tagging, and bagging all the shirts and hats for the initial launch. Our five- and seven-year-old daughters even folded a couple of shirts (until eventually they got distracted by toys).

We decided on a launch date for our website and created the bones of it. Developing a website is not simple! We used WordPress at the inception, but there was plenty of fine-tuning to make the theme, colors, and font choices feel cohesive. Keep in mind, we didn't have formal training for any of this. We were not graphic designers, fashion designers, website designers, or clothing manufacturers, but we did our best through research and development. It took many attempts to get it right. We didn't access any quick "how to start a fashion brand" e-course and didn't have a mentor guiding us through each step.

SEVERE TURBULENCE

When you are passionate and determined to do something, you just figure things out along the way and you "don't stop." As believers, I'm thankful we had Jesus to seek counsel. We prayed and consulted Him every step of the way to ask for wisdom. One thing we learned along the way was to pray and ask God to give us the *green light* to move forward. If we didn't both receive it, we didn't go through with it. I can't say we heard Him correctly on every decision or that He didn't allow us to make mistakes, but I do know His hand was and is upon us. We have felt His favor and blessing on NHiM from the beginning.

Photography

Next up was photos. We didn't want merely digital pictures or "mocks" of the shirts, sweatshirts, and hats, but instead wanted to showcase the product on real people. So we located a photographer, found some friends to be models for the brand, and arranged studio photos to make sure they looked consistent and clean. Once the photos were edited and cropped to the correct sizing for the website, we uploaded them. We then finalized the look and aesthetic for our brand's virtual platform.

We created an Instagram account and Facebook page and began a countdown for the launch of **nhimapparel.com**. We made many connections among various churches in Colorado to spread the word to as many people as possible, building anticipation for our launch day. Community and networking is essential to a new business. Having people around you who believe in you and your concept helps an idea to truly take off.

Launch Day

Our online launch day came in March of 2015. I remember sitting in front of our laptops, staring at the screen in anticipation. We posted all throughout the day on social media to bring awareness to the launch of NHiM. We texted everyone in our contacts to check out our website and consider supporting us by making a purchase. We had no idea what to expect and it was a nail-biting kind of day, waiting for the first order to come through. The first purchase came around 9 a.m., followed by a couple more from family and friends. By the end of the day, we'd sold maybe $250 online, which isn't a lot but was still something. It was enough to keep us going and believing in our pursuit.

We wanted to showcase NHiM Apparel at local events, so we signed up for craft fairs, concerts in the park, and local church events. It was vital to future customers to learn the "why" behind the brand so they could get behind wearing the logo. We attended a couple local events with a folding table, adorned with a logo banner with our website printed on it. We displayed the clothing with shirts folded and laying flat on the table. It was a basic way to start, but we didn't want to invest too heavily yet. Depending on the event, sometimes we sold $100 worth of clothing, sometimes we sold $500. But our spirits were high. The brand was getting a positive response. It was visually and aesthetically pleasing with purpose and meaning behind it. People were excited to see a Christian brand that was relevant, that they could actually see themselves wearing.

There's always a beginning to any dream — the origins, genesis, and foundations of how something gets its start. And usually it's not all that impressive. Just read the stories of some of the biggest brands out there. Before influencers on social media were commonplace, it usually took significant time to gain momentum.

As a business owner, your mindset makes all the difference. Choose to see the silver-lining, even if the initial results are minimal. Your mission is your foundation and will determine your outcome. If money is the primary motivator, then tough times or limited results will kill dreams. A dream should be a marathon and not a sprint.

 **Chapter 5**

YOU'RE FIRED

"The greatest inheritance you can pass on to your children and grandchildren is more than the money or material possessions you get. It's a legacy of both character and faith."

—Billy Graham

SEVERE TURBULENCE

I will never forget the voicemail Matt received on that Sunday afternoon. We had a busy month, preparing to sell at our biggest event yet in Colorado. "Heavenfest" was set to be the largest outdoor Christian concert event of the year. Bins and boxes of NHiM products were filling up, organized by size and style. The event was coming up at the end of the week, and we were anticipating good things. What we weren't expecting was the voicemail we received.

Matt had worked hard for 15 years at the same medical supplies manufacturer, holding the title of Vice President and General Manager. He believed he had the potential of becoming a shareholder down the road. Though it was getting increasingly difficult to juggle both his full-time job and the demands of a start-up, he had no intention of moving on from his steady paycheck just yet.

Only a few weeks before, I'd stated that I couldn't imagine him quitting his job to pursue NHiM full-time because of the risk involved. It would feel like ripping a financial security blanket off our family of five. The risk was too great. We had a sizable mortgage, car payments, and plenty of expenses. It wasn't that I didn't believe in his abilities to make NHiM work or in the brand's potential; I just couldn't see it becoming a full-time endeavor any time soon.

We were in our dining room, adding more shirts to the bins in between playing with the kids. Though there were still things to do, it felt like a relaxing and somewhat lazy Sunday afternoon. Besides, we still had several more days to get everything packed up. Matt picked up his phone and noticed he missed a call. He proceeded to listen to the voicemail left behind, and his demeanor suddenly changed. It was a message from his boss stating: "Matt, I don't need you to come in tomorrow. You'll be receiving a final paycheck with a 6-month severance option if you sign a letter of non-compete. Please sign it and return it within the week. I wish you all the best and hope you use the severance money to start your company."

He gave no explanation as to why Matt was being let go, and there was no invitation to call back and ask for further details. Instead we were handed the keys to let our minds wander. Our thoughts raced with questions. Why did this happen? And what would we do now?

It was more troubling for Matt as the sole provider, but my own fears about our financial security swirled in my mind. The following days were mentally and emotionally trying. Being let go when there's no clear-cut reason messes with your mind. Matt was flooded with mixed emotions ranging from anger, defeat, disappointment, frustration, fear, and worry, to relief and elation over the sudden freedom, and everything in between. It was unnerving. At some point in the midst of the anxiety was a very low whisper of peace. *God was giving us an opportunity.* The Word says He makes all things beautiful in His time (Eccl. 3:11) and that He works out everything for good for those who love Him (Rom. 8:28). He would make something good come from this apparent disaster.

All of our relatives advised Matt to head into Monday morning on a mission for a new job. Our parents and siblings believed there was no time to waste. They believed Matt had a husbandly and fatherly duty to find a new job immediately. The unexplainable thing was, we had no peace on that. We even considered filing for unemployment, but chose not to because it didn't feel like the right move and because we valued earning our own living. Instead, it was time to go *all in with NHiM*. This was our opportunity or gift to pursue the vision of NHiM Apparel head-on, with everything we had.

So we went for it. That next week in early August 2015, we got ready for *Heavenfest*. As we packed up our Toyota Sienna minivan full of newly printed tees, hats, stickers, our new custom tent, and other necessities, we headed to Bandimere Speedway, the famous quarter-mile racing drag strip in Morrison, Colorado. The moment we pulled up to the vendor entry spot, intimidation settled in. There were so many vendors with endless choices of Christian t-shirts and band merch (which was the main apparel pull for band groupies) and other ways to spend a dollar.

Pushing back the insecurities, we parked the van and opened up the trunk. Before I could unload anything, Matt stopped me, looked me straight in the eyes, and said, "I feel like God said in my spirit to tell everyone we meet here today that we're opening a store at Park Meadows Mall."

I was confused. Park Meadows Mall was a resort-style shopping mall in Lone Tree, Colorado, filled with high-end national brands. "What are you talking about?" I asked. "We haven't even talked to anyone about leasing at Park Meadows. We have no idea what a store would cost to rent. Isn't that untrue?"

Set on his prophetic notion, Matt told me he felt in his spirit that it was really going to happen and that we simply need to declare it to everyone we met at the event. I decided to trust him. If God was speaking to his heart about something, who was I to question that? So that's what we did.

Proverbs 18:21 says, "Death and life are in the power of the tongue, and those who love it will eat its fruit." What you declare with your mouth is of utmost importance, both in positive and negative talk. It sets the spiritual atmosphere around you. Your words either invite God's angelic armies to work on your behalf or give permission to the enemy to bring destruction.

With excitement starting to build, we set up our tent (i.e. pop-up shop) with our team of volunteers. We had a happy group of friends and family ready to volunteer. Clad in NHiM logo tees, our team immediately began passing out flyers and promotional cards to fellow vendors before the event even started. Once setup was complete, we prayed together as a team and asked God to bless the day, grant us favor, and give us peace as to whether or not we should pursue NHiM full-time.

Concert-goers began to arrive and look for food and mingle between vendors. Seemingly out of nowhere, our tent became crowded. People were asking about the brand, the story, and wanted to check out the clothes. Everyone on our team explained that we'd be opening a store in Park Meadows Mall soon, which really surprised and excited our newfound local fans. There hadn't been any Christian stores in or around the surrounding area for quite some time, so this was a big deal.

We had so many people in our tent that Matt and I struggled to complete each transaction fast enough. It was like a tidal wave. We frantically opened bins to restock or find requested sizes, pulling even the very last size off the t-shirt display to sell, with shoppers buying extra for their friends and relatives. Things were swirly in a good way, and so busy that we couldn't take a break.

By the end of the day, when it was time for vendors to tear down their display and head home, Matt and I looked at each other with the *deer in headlights* expression. Did that really just happen?? We added up sales numbers and realized we'd sold thousands in merchandise. *Thousands*. We'd never hit those kinds of numbers in one day! Plus there was a buzz and excitement in the air from everyone we met. There was evidence that NHiM had "legs" because even strangers who had never heard of the brand and didn't know us personally liked what we'd designed and created.

Honestly though, the best part of the day was the confirmation we felt in our hearts. It was as if we could see God smiling down upon us. We were experiencing what could only be described as a proud Father moment from God, as if His approval of our courage and declaration was resting over us. It was exactly the validation we needed to pursue this full-time.

Part Two

TAKEOFF

A few years before NHiM was ever envisioned, I suddenly experienced severe insomnia. Sleepless night after sleepless night, my life quickly spiraled out of control. I searched endlessly for the cause of my problem and a solution. I was desperate and miserable. I prayed continuously for God to heal me. I asked others to pray for my healing as well. I tried over-the-counter sleep medications, vitamins, supplements, and visited doctors and therapists who probed me with needles and checked for anything and everything that could be wrong. Yet nobody and nothing helped.

Was this my future? Was my life going to end this way? I was in the "prime of my life" and should've been in optimal health. There was no apparent trauma or reason for the severe insomnia. Month after month, I lost hope but clung to Jesus for a miracle. One night, after many sleepless months, I dozed off and God came to me in a dream. He said, "Matt, I am going to give you the key back to sleeping. The key for you is prayer. Stop praying only for yourself and start praying for others."

Right then, the scripture Matthew 22:36-40 popped into my mind: "Teacher, which is the most important commandment in the law of Moses?" Jesus replied, 'You must love the Lord your God with all your heart, all your soul, and all your mind. This is the first and greatest commandment. A second is equally important: 'Love your neighbor as yourself.' The entire law and all the demands of the prophets are based on these two commandments."

I woke up confused. Why would God ask me to focus on others at this time when I so desperately needed help? Why didn't He just say, "I've heard your prayers and you're healed"? Desperate, I instantly started praying. I prayed for colleagues at work, my direct family, my extended family, strangers – anyone and everyone I could think of. And then....my sleep was fully restored! But more importantly, God had called and I had answered.

Little did I know, it was the wakeup call that I needed. God was calling me into a life of service to Him. Romans 8:28 says, "**All things** work together for good, to them that love God, to them who are called according to His purpose." The dream that ended my bout of insomnia awakened me to the reality that we are all only here – living, walking, breathing – by the very hand of God. It reminded me that God has a purpose for each and every one of us. Our lives need to glorify our Creator and bring others into the awareness of Him. This introduction to the importance of praying for others (aka, intercession) came three years before the inception of NHiM. It was pivotal to what would become the foundation of the brand's mission.

If prayer was the key to my purpose, my next step was to find the doors it would unlock.

— Matt

 **Chapter 6**

KIOSK DAYS

"You will never know what you can accomplish until you say a great big yes to the Lord."

—R. G. LeTourneau

SEVERE TURBULENCE

Still feeling euphoric in the days following Heavenfest, we made some phone calls to Park Meadows Mall and spoke with the leasing company about rent options. What would it take to be able to sell at this national, resort-style mall as a start-up? Our only option was to rent a mall cart or kiosk with a six-month minimum lease. (Keep in mind, this was the most luxurious shopping mall in the area, and so there was competition to get in). They asked us to fill out paperwork and give them our sales pitch to be considered. Just days later, waiting impatiently for a reply, we got the call that they accepted us! Then they informed us what the monthly rent would be. Our jaws hit the floor. We could rent that small little cart for $5,000 a month.

Our family and parents told us not to do it. They thought it was a crazy, risky move. To assume we could sell enough clothing each month to cover rent, the cost of goods sold, and any possible employees was ludicrous in their minds. But once again, Matt and I felt we needed to give it a shot. We had an amazing opportunity to reach the community with our mission and message through NHiM.

One month following Heavenfest, we were ready to open our first physical location. It was actually happening! Our small kiosk in that giant mall may have looked humble, but we were stoked. In fact, "kiosk" may be a generous statement since it was more of a display rack with about 4' x 8' of space. Back when malls were still cool, this was the mall of dreams to hold real estate in. How would we get the attention of people passing by?

We used our NHiM Facebook page to begin building hype for our opening day. We posted a five-day countdown on Facebook, inviting all our friends, family, church acquaintances, neighbors, and anyone else we could think of to show up for the opening. The night before, we were only given a couple hours to access the kiosk for the first time and get everything set up. Our presentation was ambitious: a big-screen TV complete with a slideshow of models in our product, t-shirt mannequins for product display, and an iPad with Square checkout. Most kiosks didn't require electricity at their stand as they processed cash-only payments, but we wanted to make sure we provided all payment options so there was no reason not to close a sale.

Opening day was scheduled for September 14, 2015, and we had everything lined up. Through market research and a business mentor, we'd learned that we'd be primarily selling to females in their 30s and 40s, so we decided to carry a few items that would appeal to women in that bracket, in addition to our tees and hats. This product addition was never a part of the original vision, but with the high monthly rent we needed to set ourselves up for success. We wanted to hit on some current trends in female fashion and carry fashion accessories and even dresses (with no fitting room…) for customers to purchase alongside our NHiM branded tees. We learned it was sometimes necessary in business to create filler products to buffer sales. This was one of those moments. We quickly discovered that it was a good move.

God impressed an extremely important message upon our hearts for the grand opening. The purpose of us opening this NHiM kiosk in the mall was not to just sell some tees and make a dollar. This was *ministry*. It was a mission to bring the "church" outside its four walls and offer the hope of salvation into the secular marketplace. It was an opportunity to share the name of Jesus in an atypical way to those who needed Him. We wanted to give believers a way to wear their identity "in Him" on their clothing.

Besides, if the message of Jesus Christ stays only inside a church building, how are we reaching a lost and hurting world with the gospel? How can each of us fulfill the great commission if we stay in our church seats? We must take the message to the people, not wait for the people to come to us. Heading into this quest, we had no idea how it would be received in a mall, but we knew it needed to be our mission.

Grand opening day was a rush that even Heavenfest couldn't compete with. The morning of our opening brought so many familiar *and* unfamiliar faces to our kiosk. It was the grand opening we'd secretly dreamed of, though deep down we hadn't been sure what to expect. As people arrived, we helped groups at a time to find their size, pulling items off the shelves, out of the drawers, and ringing people up as fast as we could. We discovered that a crowd helps draw a bigger crowd. It was an incredible day and we left feeling confident that we'd followed God in pursuit of this full time.

The next day wasn't so grand. By day's end, we'd had less than ten transactions and now anxiously wondered if we'd made a bad decision by committing to this new lease. Starting a business and realizing you're at the mercy of customer traffic each day can be daunting. It's impossible to predict how your product or concept will be received by the general public. Sometimes it works out, but sometimes you do everything by the book and it just doesn't. But what was important for us was to fix our gaze on Jesus. He would guide us and give us wisdom if we asked. Whenever worry crept up, we'd do our best to talk to Jesus and remind ourselves of the mission.

The kiosk had its ups and downs. Some days reached thousands in sales, helping us cover our monthly costs, and other days had no sales. We hired one full-time employee to fill the hours that Matt and I couldn't work. Matt took the bulk of the hours so I could still primarily stay home with our kids. For non-mall hours, our time was filled with restocking products, designing new tees, bookkeeping, marketing our location, running social media, doing photo shoots, telling everyone we met about it, and so on. It was more than a full-time endeavor, but it was new and thrilling.

We also perceived a shift happening in the community. Support of NHiM grew and we started to see NHiM bumper stickers on cars, NHiM clothing in churches or in town, and shares or reshares of our posts on Facebook. Like a *fanboy*, every time we'd see someone in our clothing, we'd secretly pull out our phones to snap a picture to text to each other. We were blown away.

A couple weeks into the kiosk location, Matt felt a new pull on his heart — one that made him uncomfortable. That morning, Matt was opening the kiosk and God spoke to his heart, reminding him of his dream about praying for others. God asked Matt to start praying for each person he met at the kiosk.

Stretched out of his comfort zone, Matt got a leather book from a store in the mall, had it engraved with the words "Prayer Book," and began asking people if he could pray for them when they'd approach the kiosk. It was pretty awkward at first, yet he learned how to weave it into the conversation. He'd casually ask them if they had anything that he could pray for them about. Even if it wasn't for themselves, usually they'd find someone or something to pray for. Matt would tell them he'd pray for them, then write it down in the book after they left and pray for them. All of us staff began following suit based on this prompting by the Lord, and the prayer book quickly began filling up.

But it wasn't enough. A couple weeks later, God spoke to Matt again. He told him it was time to pray in public with the person requesting prayer, right then and there. I think they had a conversation that went a bit like this:

> *God: Matt, it's time to take the next step. I need you to pray for the people out loud.*
>
> *Matt: Wait a minute, God — I thought we were good here. I did what you asked. I took their prayer requests and I prayed for them. What more do you need from me??*
>
> *God: I want you to pray for them here and now.*
>
> *Matt: Yeah, but kiosk people are already weird! Now you want me to look even weirder to everyone walking by?? We'll be blacklisted.*
>
> *God: Just trust me, Matt.*
>
> *Matt: I don't feel qualified, I'm not a pastor.*
>
> *God: You don't need a qualification to pray for people. I've already given you the tools.*
>
> *Matt: I'll try, but I think you have the wrong person…*

Matt was super uncomfortable with this next step, and honestly so was I. I'd prayed for people at church or for friends, but more often than not I'd use the general cop-out, "I'll be praying for you." (I know you know what I'm talking about). This new kind of prayer felt like off-grid, next-level kind of stuff for us. When we first started, we stumbled through the prayer, but soon it became like second nature.

We actually loved it. And the way people responded was so encouraging. There was always some surprise when we asked to pray with them right then, but they usually left thanking us—sometimes in tears—because they were moved by the kindness of God.

Prayer is not just some combination of poetic memorized words. It's a conversation with our Creator who is bending down His ear, ready to listen. Prayer is essential to the Christian life. And prayer is the precursor to change. The Bible says, "Again I say to you that if two of you agree on earth concerning anything that they ask, it will be done for them by My Father in heaven. For where two or three are gathered together in My name, I am there in the midst of them." (Matthew 18:19-20 NKJV) As we incorporated praying aloud into our ministry-based business, we began to see change. We saw answers to prayer and it was powerful. Customers would come back to the kiosk days or weeks later, beaming, just to thank us for praying with them or to tell us that God had answered our prayer.

The word that came into Matt's heart—that we would open a store in Park Meadows Mall—had come to fruition. It was now our reality. Hearing God's voice is just the beginning; how we respond to it is everything.

KIOSK DAYS

Chapter 7

GROWING PAINS

"Our whole life is set up in the path of least resistance. We don't want to suffer. We don't want to feel discomfort. So the whole time, we're living our lives in a very comfortable area. There's no growth in that."

—David Goggins, retired US Navy Seal

SEVERE TURBULENCE

Things were running smoothly at the kiosk. We'd been open about nine months and were quickly learning that in retail there are "seasons" which create ebbs and flows in sales. For many retailers, Black Friday to Christmas brings the largest influx of shopping, with numbers that help sustain business the rest of the year. Other holidays and the start of the school year bring out more shoppers to the mall. But the middle of summer and certain weeks of the fall tend to be pretty slow in retail. Our first experience with this was sobering. Summer came and the mall was dead. We needed a bump in sales to continue covering rent, overhead, and new inventory. An idea popped in our head during the summer of 2016. How about a national tour? We decided to take the brand on the road to bring awareness to the rest of the US and ensure we could stay afloat with cash flow.

If NHiM had lasting potential, it should sell to a bigger audience beyond our local community. As a family of five, we embarked on a six-week national tour to the largest Christian music festivals around the country. This meant we'd be leaving the kiosk to operate without us for most of the summer. We had confidence in the small team of staff we'd built and planned to check-in regularly to ensure nothing fell apart.

To make this tour successful, we needed the vehicles to get us there. We found a used GMC Yukon XL and a small cargo trailer to carry the merch and tents for the events. We would need to bulk up our inventory in order to travel with enough merchandise to not sell out at each event as there wouldn't be time to restock between back-to-back events. Matt had a stellar idea to put a huge NHiM decal on the Yukon and a full wrap on the trailer to act as a *moving* billboard as we trekked across mid-America.

The travel route we mapped out would land us at large outdoor festivals like LifeFest, Elevate, Alive, Heavenfest, and Hills Alive, with a lineup of artists such as Toby Mac, NF, For King and Country, Big Daddy Weave, Colton Dixon, Newsboys, and more. To stand out from the hundreds of vendors and big tents containing band merch, we'd need to expand our pop-up storefront. We added a second custom E-Z UP tent, more display walls, additional tables, and large banners with branding and photography to catch the eye of those walking by.

We packed up and headed to our first event in Ohio. It was an outdoor event in the middle of the summer, with only a giant, open-air pavilion to house all the vendors in the 90-degree, 100% humidity temperatures. The floor was just grass and dirt, which posed problems ranging from condensation inside the poly-bags containing our tees, to shirts and hats falling off displays onto dirt, to customers placing their brightly colored slushies or funnel cakes on our table (one of which toppled over into a bin of merch), to our children needing to regularly use the only porta-potty that was 200 feet away from our busy tent.

It was a challenge. Our kids were hot and hungry on these long festival days, but we did our best to feed and care for them between busy waves of people.

But the *great* news was that the people liked NHiM. Our opportunity to test the market was working. Total strangers loved the message of the brand and the designs we sold on premium garments. And we prayed for countless people. After every event, we turned in our sales numbers at the end of the day to the event staff. Many times the event staff came back in amazement to tell us our numbers outsold the bands! Once again, we thanked God for his hand and favor upon NHiM.

As the tour continued, the summer felt long and the festival days were exhausting. Many times we arrived early in the morning and worked until nearly midnight. Our kids would fall asleep on folding chairs. It wasn't easy, but it felt like the right move at the right time to not run out of money and to maintain the brand's forward progression. We checked in regularly with the staff at the kiosk back home, and things were still running fine without us. Once August hit, we were back in Colorado and happy to be home before school started back up.

The tour helped us take our small, community-based brand to a semi-national status. Customers who purchased from us at events were now buying our product online or sharing the brand on social media with their friends. At every event, we had an iPad with an email

SEVERE TURBULENCE

newsletter sign-up form so we could acquire a bigger database for our weekly marketing. It was a summer of hustle where we chose to get uncomfortable to sustain the brand and help expand the reach of NHiM. And if we hadn't found another outlet for sales, we wouldn't have been able to cover our overhead costs at the kiosk.

Getting too comfortable doesn't give room to grow and can be the demise of a business. Discomfort is the catalyst for growth. A great piece of advice for any new business is to never get too high in the highs or too low in the lows. Don't base your future on the extremes. Renew your mind daily. (Romans 12:2). Keep your mind focused on the mission and the averages will work themselves out.

GROWING PAINS

 **Chapter 8**

THE STORE OPENS

"We cannot become what we need to be by remaining what we are."

—Max de Pree

SEVERE TURBULENCE

We'd been running the kiosk about a year and a half when the mall leasing company reached out to us with an exciting opportunity. They had noticed our sales were climbing and our brand was getting recognition. They liked what NHiM added to the mall. It was different. They informed us that a temporary store space was becoming available and wanted to know if we'd be interested in testing our brand in a physical store.

We had to pause and take it all in. This was a big deal for us – it was something we'd envisioned and hoped for, but weren't ready for. One caveat was that the buildout would have to be done by a professional, licensed contractor and fully approved by the mall. Remember, this was a luxury shopping resort that required a certain image to be represented in each of their storefronts. Our temporary store couldn't look temporary, so it would be yet another significant investment. The rent would also be about double what we were paying for the kiosk. But it would provide us with 3,500 square feet of space and a greater potential to be seen by indoor mall traffic.

3,500 square feet….How would we go from a 32-square-foot kiosk to a 3,500-square-foot store?!? We needed way more inventory and variety to fill it up. It was a huge undertaking. The timing was potentially a great opportunity too, as the store would open a few weeks before Black Friday, with increased holiday traffic. The leasing team couldn't give us any guarantees as to how long we could be in the space, but they assured us it would most likely be longer than just the holiday season. The mall also typically only allowed national tenants to be in a storefront, so it was uncharted waters for both them and us.

We prayed about it and felt peace to go for it. We hired a friend, a general contractor, who offered us a reduced rate to help us turn the space into a fully functioning clothing store complete with dressing rooms, a large checkout counter, custom display tables, and a plan to optimize the merchandising areas. We got busy creating graphics for new tees, adding more NHiM accessories, adding jewelry, and bulking up the selection of boutique-style clothing for women. We mapped out the store to determine clothing displays, a lounge area, placement of the checkout counter, and flow of the space.

By November 1, 2016, we closed down the kiosk for good and opened up our first brick and mortar store. It was a big day! About an hour before opening, the items were set and the custom playlist we'd curated could be heard on the newly installed Bose sound system. NHiM signage was strewn throughout the store and window displays were looking *on point* with large decorative light bulbs hung like a garland. We'd prayed with our enthusiastic team full of new faces. We were all in high spirits, ready to greet our potential new customers.

Then it hit us. It was all for this moment. The sum of events leading up to this day came into my mind like a movie on a reel. The dream Matt had years earlier about how to end his bout with insomnia through prayer for others was so significant. This was a door that the key of prayer was opening. God had given us this opportunity to be a light in the marketplace. Just as Paul did ministry in the marketplace of Athens, we were walking into full-time ministry with a Kingdom-based business whose sole purpose was to reach people with the gospel through apparel and to offer prayer in the marketplace. Reality was settling in. A Bible verse had become a logo. That logo had evolved into a brand. What began in a tent had become a kiosk, and now a store.

Somewhere around 30 minutes before the grand opening, people started showing up. A line began to form outside the front windows of the store. As many as 25 people were lined up, waiting to come into the NHiM store. We couldn't believe it. In shock and disbelief, we again thanked God for his goodness. Matt and I grabbed the large handles of the double doors and said, "Ready?" and together opened the doors. It was an incredible opening day as we interacted with all the regulars and newcomers to the NHiM brand. The thrill and excitement from the customers was on par with our level of enthusiasm. It was another monumental milestone.

You may be wondering, why t-shirts and prayer in the mall? When God first spoke to us about praying with people in the mall, we didn't know if this would be the model we'd continue building on or if it would just be a step of faith for our personal growth. But as we walked in obedience to God's voice, we realized this was God's design for our brand. The more we prayed with people in public, the more He taught us how to lean into His voice during prayer. We'd see or hear His heart for people and discern what to pray over them. Becoming a person of prayer doesn't take a seminary degree or ministry position—it simply takes time in His presence. The more time we spend with Jesus as we partner with Him in prayer, the more we learn to pray the things in His heart, not just the things in ours.

Weeks before the grand opening, we'd been interviewing new faces to add to our growing team. The most important interview questions to us were:

1. Tell us about your history and relationship with Jesus.
2. How's your prayer life?
3. Are you comfortable praying in public or willing to learn?

That was it. Sure, there were other factors that came into play with any potential staff member, but our primary goal was to hire staff who loved the Lord and loved to pray. Being an outgoing person was also a plus, but above all else we wanted to ensure our staff knew how to pray.

As the store became established, prayer took root in our identity. It was powerful to watch so many people receiving prayer and encouragement from our amazing staff. Before mall opening hours, we had regular Bible studies with our team, worshiped together, and prayed for one another. NHiM was really taking off. It seemed like the only way was up. In our eyes, nothing could go wrong. Only time would tell what kind of clouds lie ahead on the journey.

THE STORE OPENS

Chapter 9

DREAMS & VISIONS

"All our dreams can come true, if we have the courage to pursue them."

—Walt Disney

SEVERE TURBULENCE

Before the dream of NHiM ever took flight, God was preparing our hearts. He had to train us and give us vision for the runway. I remember many dreams I had before we launched our brand that came into play later on. I've always been a dreamer. Since I was young, I could recall many dreams from the night before and explain them in detail after I awoke. I assumed everyone dreamed as vividly as I did, so I didn't think anything of it. But as I've gotten older I've become more aware of the differing ways God speaks to each of us, which has made me pay closer attention to dreams.

God clearly gives people dreams throughout the Bible. Acts 2:17 and Joel 2:28 says, "In the last days, God says, I will pour out my Spirit on all people. Your sons and daughters will prophesy, your young men will see visions, your old men will dream dreams." Dreams serve as a tool for many purposes. Some dreams are instructional, like in the story of Joseph and Mary in Matthew Chapter 2. Dreams can also be correctional, like in Genesis Chapter 20 with Abraham. Daniel in the Bible received dreams and visions of future events to come (see Daniel chapters 7-12).

In our lives, God has spoken to us through dreams mostly through analogies of something we'd come to experience at some point in the future. Most mornings, I can remember certain parts of a dream I had the previous night, but when a dream seems surreal or I wake up in the middle of it with full clarity, I pay attention. Sometimes I've awoken and immediately known it was a dream from the Lord. About a year before we started NHiM, I had one of those dreams.

In the dream, Matt and I were driving his black Jeep Wrangler on an undeveloped piece of land near an intersection. (Side note—I loved that Jeep). We stepped out of the car onto the uneven dirt landscape and looked up to see an odd and unbelievable sight. It appeared that something in Earth's atmosphere was shifting—the Sun turned black, the stars were falling, and everything was swirling above us.

A voice spoke from the Heavens. It was the voice of God, who said in a calm yet booming voice, "The end is near. I want you to go and tell as many people as you can. Tell them to repent and turn back to me." As soon as we heard this, we began running on foot to share the gospel. Oddly enough, we didn't run to the streets, but straight into churches. As we entered each church, we saw congregations of people standing up, yet fully asleep. We ran from person to person, grabbing their shoulders, shaking them and telling them to "WAKE UP! TURN BACK TO GOD!" They began waking up and fully surrendering to the Lord. At that point, I woke up from the dream and knew it was from the Lord. I may not have grasped the meaning of it, but it was a marking dream.

When Jesus spoke to crowds He used parables, or stories. I believe God speaks to us this way many times in dreams. Not everything in a dream is always as literal as it seems and the meaning may not be evident at first, but through prayer and revelation, we can uncover what God is speaking to us. I prayed off and on for years to understand what this specific dream meant, but didn't hear an answer. It wasn't until a couple years into our NHiM journey that this dream came back to me with greater understanding.

Though I'd forgotten all about it, the dream resurfaced while we were in our brick-and-mortar store location in Park Meadows Mall. We were fully immersed in our Kingdom-based business and had a mentality to do whatever it took to keep things running. Customers were coming in regularly to shop or just get prayer. We had become a hub outside the local church where people felt safe to share the areas they needed prayer for, such as healing or breakthrough. We had a staff filled with the Holy Spirit, fired up to love on people and pass out hope in the heart of Colorado.

Near Christmastime, an acquaintance came into our store. She was a missionary living in Costa Rica who had come back home to Colorado for the holidays. The virtuous work she was doing in Costa Rica was to rescue victims of human trafficking. It was no easy feat and required a lot of prayer and persistence.

On her way home, she sent us an email about her experience visiting our store. She shared that she was walking the hallways of Park Meadows Mall and could feel in her spirit the darkness and corruption

SEVERE TURBULENCE

in the atmosphere. She was talking to the Lord about it as she walked the mall and then came upon our store. As she did, she had a vision that God's light was flooding out of its doors. She felt God saying that our store was bringing hope to people and that the message of the Gospel was lighting up the darkness. She explained that she saw people walking around asleep and we at NHiM were *waking them up* from their slumber.

When I read that in the email, I was wrecked by God's love. I remembered the dream God had given me years before about awakening those who were spiritually asleep. I was so thankful that Jesus, in His kindness, had shown us a prior glimpse of the powerful hope and message of the gospel that we would be able to release in a secular marketplace. It was the affirmation Matt and I needed to remind ourselves that we weren't just selling clothing. The product was God's love. The "why" was the hope of the Gospel. We had to keep blazing a trail.

DREAMS & VISIONS

 **Chapter 10**

A HOME FOR 12 ANGELS

"I alone cannot change the world, but I can cast a stone across the waters to create many ripples."

—Mother Teresa

SEVERE TURBULENCE

Several years ago, I'd learned that India had one of the largest populations of orphans anywhere in the world. Thirty million small children—including toddlers—live in dumps, fending for themselves daily, eating rancid food out of trash cans and alleyways, fighting daily against diseases to stay alive. Many orphans do not live to see their eighteenth birthday. On top of this, having no one to watch over them leads to child trafficking and exploitation, or being forced to join violent extremist groups. No child should be faced with these types of dire situations.

Knowing what these children were going through was heartbreaking. But more than that, the knowledge made Matt and I feel responsible. We had to do something to help. After several discussions, we decided to take a portion of every NHiM sale and set it aside to build an orphanage. We partnered with a non-profit organization called Angel House, which had already built over 200 homes to rescue orphans off the streets in India. We wanted to personally provide one more—and with Black Friday just under our belt, we were on pace to do so. We had more sales in that one weekend than we could have ever anticipated. The holiday sales combined in our new store nearly exceeded an entire year of sales at the kiosk! From the proceeds of the Black Friday sales, we were able to finally pay for a new, fully furnished orphanage for 12 children to be rescued off the streets of India.

On December 5, 2016, Matt and I eagerly boarded Flight QR708 from Washington D.C. to Doha, India. (Sound familiar? Yes, it's the same turbulent flight described in Chapter 1.) We never could have imagined the traumatic experience we were about to endure! The turbulence was incredibly intense, and when the plane began to plummet and shake, everything became surreal. Chaos erupted around us, and the thought of this being our last moments on earth was at the forefront of our minds. All we could do was pray.

And then, something began to shift. After what seemed like an eternity, the pilot seemed to regain some control of the plane and the turbulence finally began to slowly settle. We were so rattled, yet incredibly thankful that whatever had just happened might be over.

The flight attendants tended to the injured, and two passengers in the medical field provided care to the man who had experienced the heart attack. The pilot and flight crew remained silent, leaving all of us travelers in the dark as to why this happened and what would happen next. Finally, the pilot announced that he would be dropping fuel for an emergency landing. Just when I'd started to calm down, a new wave of fear set in. I looked at the digital map on the screen in front of me and saw only the ocean. Where would we land?? Was the plane severely damaged or was there something else we did not know? Would we survive the descent?

Questions swirled through my mind until the pilot came back on the loudspeaker to announce that we were beginning our descent. We would land in the Azores, a small chain of Portuguese islands in the middle of the Atlantic Ocean, with more cows than people. Finally, after descending amidst heavy sideways rain and wind, we landed on Lajes Field on the island of Terceira. The entire plane erupted in cheers and applause when the wheels touched down. As people who'd just escaped death, we thanked God extravagantly, over and over again, that we were safely on land. Before anyone deplaned, the local medics boarded the plane to take care of the injured passengers. We were so grateful to be on the ground. We joyfully hugged the other passengers, doing our best to shake off the shocking ordeal we'd all just endured.

Nearly 36 hours later—after making our way through immigration and customs, we white-knuckled another plane ride off the island of Terceira to our intended destination of Doha. It never occurred to us then that this very experience would be the inception of a book that would parallel our experience of turbulence with the pursuit of the dream of NHiM. Relieved to be out of the air and on the ground, we crammed into a narrow bus to embark on an hour-long journey from the city of Hyderabad in south-central India, to the tiny town of Ibrahimpatnam. Seeing those kids smile would be worth all the trauma we had endured on our flight there.

We rode down bumpy back roads at uncomfortable speeds, sweating in the stifling hot air. Car horns went off every couple of seconds and we passed by many things I'd never seen, from free-roaming street monkeys to entire families riding on the back of a motorcycle. An hour felt like forever—and yet suddenly, we arrived. We were just moments away from meeting these 12, beautiful children.

Stepping off the bus into the small village was surreal. I gazed upon the small church that sat as the foundation our orphanage was built on top of. It wasn't like any church I'd ever seen in America. It was about the size of a small garage, poorly constructed out of cement with metal rods still protruding from the unfinished concrete edges. Compared to American standards, it was practically unpermitted to be called a church, and certainly wouldn't meet any building codes, but it was a *lighthouse*. Sitting on the outskirts of town, it was the only Christian church in this small Hindu agricultural village.

For the past 20 years, the female pastor of this church, Ravi, had been tirelessly doing the work of God, reaching her community with the gospel, all on her own. And if that wasn't enough, her heart ached for the orphans. She began taking in abandoned children she found off the streets of this poor town into the church, mothering them and caring for their basic needs. She had limited funds, with no beds or rooms to give them, and no funding for backpacks or school supplies—which was a requirement in order to attend school. She needed an actual home, kitchen, furniture, and financial help to care for these children and provide proper shelter for them.

I could feel the gravity of the gift they were receiving that day. I knew that these children and adoptive mother had experienced the favor of God through our simple "yes" to God. It was humbling to think that simply giving back a portion of our profits from NHiM could make such a massive difference in the lives of these children all the way across the world—children that I would never have met or known about otherwise. I had to take a moment to pause, to thank God and let it all sink in.

As we greeted them all and saw their sweet little faces, our hearts melted. By the end of the day, my face hurt from smiling so much. Their joy was infectious despite their lack. The day was spent with

A HOME FOR 12 ANGELS

more hugs than I could count, playing games with these kids, teaching them worship songs in English, praying over them, and gifting them with new clothes including an NHiM shirt, shoes, toys, and backpacks with school supplies. It was like Christmas—and not just for them. Our hearts were overflowing with joy as we got back into the bus that evening.

Opening that home, meeting the children, and spending the day with them was something I will never forget or take for granted. I'm so thankful that we could pour into the lives of these children, the church, and Ravi to build them a complete home. The home provided them each with their own beds, plus two bathrooms, a living space, kitchen area, courtyard for play, and a clean water well. We were even able to help finish the building project of the church below the home.

God is so unbelievably good. He is the Great Provider. He makes a way when there seems to be no way. When we bring justice to the fatherless, God delights in it because love is His language. James 1:27 says, "Religion that God our Father accepts as pure and faultless is this: to look after orphans and widows in their distress and to keep oneself from being polluted by the world."

As we traveled to different cities within the state of Telangana, there was a lot to process. Seeing the level of poverty in villages and small towns near Hyderabad put a lot of things into perspective about what is and what isn't important in life. It's said that two-thirds of India lives on less than $2 a day. As an American, it's hard to even comprehend what that would be like. Think about the last purchase you made without blinking an eye that probably cost far more than $2.

We completed other mission work while in India, allowing us to meet many faces along the way. Near one of the other orphanages we helped open, small huts lined the streets. A woman waved at us from one of the huts and began motioning to come see her. The glow on her face was infectious. She radiated with joy as she showed us her humble home made from tarps. It was hard to equate her happy disposition with her meager living situation, but I didn't have time to think about it for too long.

SEVERE TURBULENCE

"Come in, come in," she said in Telugu (the native language) as she motioned to us to enter her home and admire what she'd built with her own two hands. She had been sweeping with a homemade broom before we walked up. The home was probably about five feet wide and maybe another four to six feet in length with just enough room over our heads to walk inside. The roof and walls were constructed of black tarps, with poles holding the structure up and rope keeping it all together. It was similar to a camping tent with a flat top. There was no floor, just dirt. The only furnishings were a small rug, a cot woven from twine, and a few pots and pans.

Not much of what you'd expect in a home, yet she was so incredibly proud. I felt ashamed of what I'd come to expect of a home with my privileged American standards, but I kept my emotions underwrap. I didn't want to take anything away from the joy we were sharing. Though we couldn't communicate in the same language, there was still mutual love and support for each other. I kept smiling and hugged her, thanking her for her cheerful hospitality to show us her home. She lit up our day.

Another day during our trip, we went to a village to open a home that would house special needs teens and young adults. The group of disowned young people had been living in unsuitable conditions with two loving house parents who had taken them off the streets and were caring for them. Being born with a disability is shameful in the Hindu religion as it is seen as the 'karma' or result of punishment from a past life of sin. Due to this, many children with disabilities are shunned from their families in India and sometimes become excommunicated or abandoned by their parents. It's heartbreaking. This particular group had been living in a ground-level home that was too small and also dangerous. In this particular area of Southern India, there were many poisonous snakes that could make their way into a ground-level home, which had caused near-fatal snake bites to some of them. They were desperately in need of safe living conditions.

A celebration was coming the day of the new home opening. The local women in the village made a cake for the big opening. The young adults and everyone around them were so excited. As the cake was being passed out, some of the kids and young adults had a hard time eating it because of the impairment of their fine motor skills or varying disabilities. While most were enjoying their slice of cake, I noticed that one young man who had cake in front of him wasn't eating it. I asked one of the house parents why, and she told me his hands didn't work properly. (In India, you eat with your hands, not forks). My heart was sad for him. She told me that I could feed him, but then it dawned on me that she meant with my hands!

I was uncomfortable, but I knew I needed to get past the awkwardness on my part. I looked at Matt, who smiled and encouraged me to go ahead. I picked up a piece of the cake between my thumb and pointer finger and placed it in the man's mouth. He smiled so big that it filled my heart up. He was so happy to be eating birthday cake that it made me realize how silly my initial discomfort was. I was glad to help another one of God's children who was so loved by our Heavenly Father. As I fed him cake, I was once again reminded of my own health that I had to be grateful for. We left the home at sunset and headed back to where we were staying, reflecting on all the new experiences we had that day. To see the heart of God and to be his 'literal' hands and feet was an honor.

Mission trips can knock you out of the bubble most of us live in. One of the most impactful moments on a mission trip is when your own sense of reality gets a wake up call. Witnessing poverty, challenging living conditions, or people who need the hope of the Gospel is sobering. I'm learning more and more throughout the years to not value my own comfort or provision over God.

The encounter we had with the beautiful people of India was another line in the sand for me. As we made our way back to Colorado, we reflected on our trip. Our time there made us want to continue to give generously and without restraint, and to share His message of love while looking at the world through His lens. All it takes is a simple "yes." Any world issue can seem daunting, but God is only asking us each to do our part in whatever it is that he calls us to help in. And

SEVERE TURBULENCE

God has a big heart for orphans.

May we never let the enormity of a problem prevent us from acting upon the pull in our heart for change. Whatever God is prompting you to do, use the age old Nike slogan and 'just do it.'

For more information on how to get involved in helping orphaned children in India, visit https://angelhouse.me/

A HOME FOR 12 ANGELS

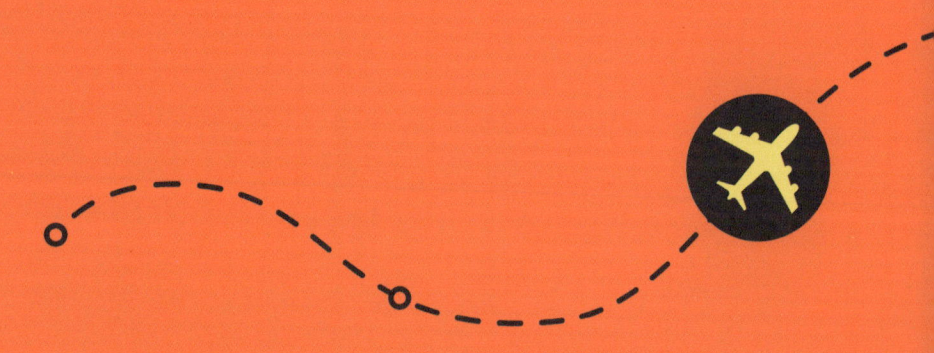

Part Three
UNEXPECTED TURBULENCE

It took a couple years for Diane and I to overcome the post-trauma left over in our memory banks after that terrifying flight to India. Thankfully, God used it as a character-defining moment for our family, a so-called 'blueprint' of how to get from point A to point B in any circumstance, holding onto faith throughout the turbulence. He showed us how to look to Him in suffocating moments, when the flight path is rough and the ETA unknown.

Are you familiar with the story of Joseph from the Bible? He was a 17-year-old shepherd boy who was the favored child to his father. You might remember him as the guy with the "coat of many colors." God had given him dreams of becoming a great ruler, but his brothers were jealous and secretly hated him. After Joseph told them about his dreams of greatness, they hated him even more and plotted to kill him. One day while Joseph was looking for his brothers in the pasture, they threw him into an empty cistern and left him to die.

I can only imagine that this was a "severe turbulence" type of moment for Joseph. Thoughts of panic must've raced through his mind as he feared that he could be living his last days. Yet shortly after the brothers left Joseph to die, they saw some travelers and decided to instead sell Joseph into slavery for 20 pieces of silver. The travelers then resold Joseph to Potiphar, an officer of Pharaoh in Egypt, and he spent the next 13 years either serving Potiphar or imprisoned by false accusations.

It wasn't until age 30 that Joseph was released from prison. He went from a prisoner to a ruler overnight, set to rule as second in command over the land of Egypt. Everything he "touched" turned to gold; in other words, God miraculously blessed all he put his hand to. His former God-given dreams would only then begin to be fulfilled, so many years later. Joseph persevered in the hardship, with the hope of the promises to come, and demonstrated **undeterred faith** in the waiting.

Joseph is a prime example of a man who didn't give up on the promises God spoke to him in a dream. Though he went through devastation and intense trials before being promoted, he kept the vision God gave him in his dream at the forefront of his mind. He humbly served and honored those around him, worked hard in all he put his hand to, and never gave up, even while he was imprisoned.

I often think of the story of Joseph when life is challenging. This hero of the faith can teach us to always remember the vision God places before us and to never give up, even when things feel impossible.

— Matt

 **Chapter 11**

AN UPSIDE-DOWN KINGDOM

"Success is not final; failure is not fatal: it is the courage to continue that counts."

—Winston Churchill

SEVERE TURBULENCE

After arriving back home from India, our spirits were high. We couldn't wait to get back and share all the good news with our staff. Yet as soon as we came back, that high was brought to a new low. The mall sent us a letter saying we had to vacate the new storefront in 15 days. What?! We'd been in our new storefront for less than two months, invested nearly $75,000 in the buildout, and now we had to move out? It felt like the drop in the plane ride, the *pit-in-our-stomach* type of news after having such a great start. Customer enthusiasm and sales were soaring, but the loss of the buildout cost negated any profit.

At first, the mall only offered for us to go back into a kiosk space. That was beyond disheartening and humiliating. There was no way we wanted to go backwards after this step forward. But the mall had signed a long-term lease agreement with a national tenant and needed us out. After many pleading conversations and failed negotiations, the mall unenthusiastically offered us a new 1,000-square-foot space with a five-month temporary contract. They simply preferred national, long-term tenants. We were fighting an uphill battle.

Going from a big space to a small space meant that everything had to be reworked. The large amount of remaining inventory would need to be displayed in a creative, space-saving way in order to fit. We had custom-built everything for the previous store—dressing rooms, check-out counter, lounge area, display tables, and more—and none of it would fit in the new space. Saving money and cutting costs was now our focus. For clothing displays, we went with a minimalist modern style, using black industrial steel piping and stripping the outer coating to achieve a gray steel look, and fitting the pipes together with caps and wall anchors. With the help of an amazing team of people, we moved overnight, finishing up around three in the morning so we could open the next day during mall hours. It was fast and furious, but we were determined not to miss being open.

The first couple weeks and months went well enough. We did our best to communicate to our customers that we weren't closed or gone, but that we'd just moved across the hallway. Most customers missed the original space (as did we), but we had to make the best of our new smaller store. We continued having frequent Bible studies and a time of worship with our team before mall hours and continued to pray to have an impact on anyone passing by in the mall or entering our store. We also prayed that we could become a permanent storefront in the mall, as this was still only a temporary lease (which was now extremely expensive). The crazy thing is that our monthly rent doubled again after moving into the new, much smaller space, as we had been getting a "deal" for filling an empty store during the holidays. With that kind of rent number to pay each month, we had to ensure our store met its daily sales goals so we didn't lose money.

As the end of the five-month temporary lease approached, Matt kept reaching out to the mall management and leasing team to enter into a permanent contract. They kept telling us no. They were worried we didn't have what it took to survive in the mall since we weren't a national tenant and couldn't pull in the traffic that other well-known brands did. They saw our monthly sales numbers and told us we weren't selling enough. Call it what you want, but we weren't satisfied with that answer. Matt did everything in his power to convince them, while they kept telling us no. We began to pray as a team that God would move on our behalf and allow us to remain in the mall. We believed there was a purpose for us to be there, beyond selling clothing. We were "clothing" others with the hope of the Gospel, and we couldn't just give up and close our doors.

After weeks of praying, we got an email saying they would consider changing their decision if we signed a three-year contract, gave them a deposit equal to three months of (even higher) rent, and hired an architect to build out the store to look as professional and top-notch as the national brands in the mall. We agreed and signed the permanent lease! We found an architect—a friend of a friend who came highly recommended—to design our storefront for a permanent buildout. It was another giant leap of faith and our biggest investment yet.

For the redesign, we wanted a clean, modern look, so we chose a Scandinavian-style build, using pegboard floating panels in light colored pine wood on black painted walls. The new panels would need to be custom made from a high-end furniture maker using large sheets of premium high-gloss wood, then CNC machined to create precisely drilled holes for the giant pegboard system. This would look both sleek and modern and allow wood dowels to be inserted for a variety of clothing display options. The architect designed the store to have the checkout counter in the center to optimize the product display on the walls along with wood dressing rooms and doors (as opposed to the curtains we previously had hanging). It was absolutely beautiful and so different from anything else in the mall.

The investment of the total build was upwards of $150,000. It was money we didn't have and needed to acquire a loan for. With the investment, we had high hopes our sales would naturally increase too. It took a couple months to build the wall panels, checkout counter, display racks, new lighting, and sound system. We then closed our doors for about two weeks while everything was installed. We were stoked. It was the grand opening, all over again. We had another celebratory opening day and lots of new support. Our customers loved the new look of the store, but in the back of our minds we wondered: would the investment pay off?

Word got around and our store became a staple for Christians in Colorado. More and more cars touted our NHiM logo decal on their back window, doing their part to share the brand with others on the road. We were known for prayer in the marketplace and relevant designs that Christians wanted to wear. We regularly designed new products for the brand and continued carrying clothing specific to women as well. We even added home decor and athletic wear with powerful statements of faith.

One thing God taught us early on in the process: ***never focus on sales.*** He was teaching us the "upside-down Kingdom" mentality. Every time we stressed about the sales or worried about paying rent, we'd have a team huddle and talk to our staff about how to try harder with customers, suggest other products, or help our guests "shop" so that we'd increase our numbers. Yet every time we did that, our sales were worse! So then Matt and I would ask God, "What are we doing wrong??" And He'd always remind us that the mission of NHiM was not about the money. He'd tell us to instead focus on prayer and loving people well.

You see, God's kingdom is upside-down from the ways of this world. The last shall be first, the first shall be last. We aren't meant to do things the way the world does them because that doesn't work in God's kingdom. Jesus modeled a very different way of life than everyone expected. So we shouldn't expect anything less than different when God gives us insight into His ways.

So we switched tactics and told the team to simply love on people, pray with them, show compassion, and share Jesus with everyone who came in. And that's when we'd see a sales increase. It was never the other way around! We tend to listen better to His voice when we really need His help, right?! So that became our first focus. Not the sales, not the clothes, but just giving the love of Jesus to every person who walked in our doors.

Our team continued to grow. It was beautiful to watch our staff develop in ministry. We witnessed those who were initially uncomfortable praying for others become prayer warriors. They gained discernment for people in prayer and received words from the Lord to share. We saw many healings and answered prayers in our store.

At one point we hired our nephew, Levi, to create a short video to film testimonies from our customers. We'd been hearing that many people were receiving answers to the prayers they'd received in our store. We sent an email out, asking if anyone had a testimony to share about their experience. The hope was to use the video as a way to glorify God for how He'd been moving at NHiM. The outcome was staggering. We set up a camera after mall hours and almost 100 people showed up that night to share their testimonies! The line wrapped from our store down the hallway and almost to the doors that led outside the mall. We could not believe it. We were so amazed at how God was using simple, genuine prayers. His goodness amazed us.

In the process of growth for NHiM, we'd been facing our own

internal struggle. There was a newfound stirring in our hearts that we didn't know what to do with. For a couple of years, we'd been struggling to find the level of spiritual growth we hoped for on Sundays in a church. We didn't deeply connect with any of the local churches in Colorado. We regularly served on Sunday mornings, but left feeling empty. Church felt more like a fun social club than a place of spiritual growth and worship. It wasn't that they weren't moral places with communities of Jesus-loving people; it was that they felt spiritually asleep, like in my dream.

We loved living in Colorado and being near extended family and a circle of amazing friends, but something was missing. We were hungry for a move of God – not only in our own lives, but corporately in a church body. There was a spiritual apathy in the air that we couldn't shake. It was nothing against the spiritual climate in Colorado, but simply a call on our lives personally. A few months prior, we had visited a church in Redding, California that had made a lasting impact on us. Now it felt like the spirit of God was drawing us back.

It was time to pray about our next leap of faith.

AN UPSIDE-DOWN KINGDOM

Chapter 12

WEST COAST MOVE

"We keep moving forward, opening new doors, and doing new things, because we're curious and curiosity keeps leading us down new paths."

—Walt Disney

SEVERE TURBULENCE

Matt and I tried to hide our excitement and emotions after visiting Redding, California to see our good friends, but we couldn't hold it in. We had been looking for God's direction for the next season of our lives, but weren't sure when that would come or what it would look like. During our visit to Redding, we attended an evening service at Bethel Church and experienced an eye-opening prophetic word for the first time. I knew very little about the prophetic gift mentioned in the Bible and honestly didn't understand how normal people used it in modern-day times. Were there really ordinary people who just happened to be filled with the Holy Spirit?

We attended a powerful service with an incredible time of worship. There was a peace in the atmosphere that I'd never felt before. God's presence was truly tangible and our hearts filled with joy. As the service came to a close, the leaders extended an invitation to come to the front for a prayer line. Those ministering said a quick prayer or word of encouragement as people walked down the line.

Matt and I decided to go up to the front and began walking down the line, receiving prayer. The ministers knew nothing about us personally, yet some spoke truths and declarations over us that were very accurate. We saw senior Pastor Bill Johnson in line and hoped to get prayer from him, but he was busy with another leader. When we got to the end of the prayer line, a man with a huge smile asked us if we were married and if he could give us a word. His name was Joel. He told us God gave him a very specific word for us.

As he began to share what God was telling him, it was like our hearts were wide open and bare for all to see. It was as if he was seeing into our very lives. He literally read our mail. I'd never before experienced something so personal like this—that God valued our hearts so much to speak through a messenger to bring us direction and encouragement. He even had a revelation of the number and ages of our children and shared a calling on one of our children's lives that had been evident to us. He shared the symbolism of the past season we'd come out of and the future hope of the ministry and movement we were building. It was a truly remarkable moment.

That's how deeply our Father loves us. When we take the time to seek more of Him, He will take the time to let us know that He sees and hears us, and that He's building a bright and beautiful future for us. I fully believe God moves through the prophetic and that it's used for the edification and encouragement of His followers today.

Take a look at what the Bible says about it in 1 Corinthians 12:7-11:

> "A spiritual gift is given to each of us so we can help each other. To one person the Spirit gives the ability to give wise advice; to another the same Spirit gives a message of special knowledge. The same Spirit gives great faith to another, and to someone else the one Spirit gives the gift of healing. He gives one person the power to perform miracles, and another the ability to prophesy. He gives someone else the ability to discern whether a message is from the Spirit of God or from another spirit. Still another person is given the ability to speak in unknown languages, while another is given the ability to interpret what is being said. It is the one and only Spirit who distributes all these gifts. He alone decides which gift each person should have."

That night marked us. The prophetic word we received fueled our hearts with renewed purpose and a reminder that God had not forgotten us. It gave us insight into His plans for us, telling us that we were building much more than we could see in the here and now. That someday we would leave a legacy if we continued to pursue Him without abandon. For us, this meant uprooting our lives and moving to California to be a part of a church that was unlike anything we'd experienced before. All we wanted was simply more of Jesus.

The Big Move

Fast-forward a month later. We came back for one more visit to Redding to look for a home. We were moving from the beautiful, upper-class, perfectly planned city of Castle Rock to a town that looked very different from what we were used to. On the surface, it was an agricultural town that didn't seem very spectacular, but it was filled with some of the most interesting people we'd ever met. We met people who were building businesses, ministries, and movements. They were people who weren't afraid to dream big ideas that seemed unrealistic to attain. A couple who later became dear friends had started a successful business based completely off of "blueprints" that God gave them in a dream. Never in my life had I heard of that. Most people went to college for that kind of business plan and idea!

We were there on the prospect to own land for the first time—a dream in our hearts—and to find a home that was move-in ready. We met with a realtor and looked at some homes, but didn't fall in love with anything. Matt ended up flying out to Redding once more and finding a property that wasn't in the listings our realtor had shown us. He FaceTimed me with barely any cell service and showed me our future home—should God make a way. It felt like a retreat, with a 22-acre park-like setting. We had never owned even one acre, so it would be a big life change!

Though we were excited to make the move, it was also scary. We'd be leaving our entire life behind. We'd been in Colorado most of our lives and almost all of our family lived there. We also had really close friends that we'd be sad to leave. I'd been a worship leader for years and would be stepping down to make this move. Plus, all of our children had been raised in our home in Castle Rock from the time they were babies, and so many memories were housed there. It was hard to think about leaving it all behind. But we knew that if we never left our hometown, we'd always wonder if we had missed out on something. Call us adventurous, I guess! We were following God's direction and had to trust Him with the rest of it.

We made an offer on the new home, contingent upon ours selling within 14 days. It wasn't much time to get our home listed and find the right buyer. What happened next was a miracle. On the very last night of our contingency, when all other offers had fallen through, we got a call from our realtor at 10 p.m. telling us that "Jesus" bought our house!

Okay, it may not have been Jesus as in Christ, but it was a person with the name Jesus. All we could do was laugh at God's incredible humor and praise and thank Him for His provision. Isn't it always like God to test our characters to see if we trust Him as provider? Sometimes it's in the "midnight hour" that He comes through. And in that instance it was.

Moving Day

We'd been given a quote over the phone to move our family cross-country. Based off our square footage and belongings, the $4,000 estimate sounded reasonable, so we didn't give it further thought. But on moving day, after the trucks pulled up to our home and the crew walked through and did their assessment, they came back outside to inform us it would now cost $16,000 instead. They said they accidentally misquoted us.

I thought it had to be a joke. We hadn't set that kind of money aside! Meanwhile, Matt did all he could to negotiate with the movers to try to get the price down. They agreed to a slightly lower rate, *if we would also rent a large U-haul and move a third of it ourselves.* What a mess! We ended up needing financial help from family to cover the cost. It was a stressful day with a lot of tension. It was so stressful, in fact, that I didn't see my prized Taylor guitars make their way onto the moving truck before I could put them in our car for safekeeping.

We made it to Redding in mid-September of 2018. The road there was so challenging that it made us question our decision and newfound direction from God quite a few times after we arrived in California. We closed on our new home by the skin of our teeth, due to an overlooked additional $60,000 solar loan tied to the home. About a week later, the movers showed up to our new address and began unloading items. I noticed one of our accent tables had been damaged in the move with a busted cabinet door, and one of our high-top stools had a broken leg. Although I was a little disappointed, I thought things went pretty well overall.

The next day I was moving things around and noticed my guitars were put in a weird corner of a room, so I moved them into what would become our music room. I saw that the outside of one of the hard cases was damaged. It was almost like a chunk had come off the edge of the case. The other hard shell case had a broken latch as well. I started to get that sick feeling in my stomach at the thought of what I was going to find when I opened the cases.

I pulled my Signature Series Jewel guitar out of the case and saw the giant double cracks down both sides of the guitar body. It was totally destroyed. I cried and almost couldn't catch my breath. It was the first guitar I'd bought at 20 years of age when I began leading worship. I grabbed the other case, which held my valuable Taylor K24ce acoustic guitar, made of Hawaiian koa wood and given to me as a gift from Matt. I opened it to discover that the bottom of the guitar was smashed and severe damage had been done to the face. Flooded with shock and disbelief, my tears began to flow.

I felt like I had just been robbed. Like a child, I sat on the floor, heartbroken and crying for nearly an hour. As a worship leader for most of my adult life, I felt like I had already given up so much by moving away and leaving it behind for a season. I would no longer be leading worship regularly as we settled into a new church home, and now this? It wasn't even just the broken guitars that hurt so badly. It was a representation of my worship to God. Although I had given up leading worship corporately for a season, I'd comforted myself knowing that at least I would have my guitars to worship the Lord in the quiet place. But now they were totally unusable. I felt like the enemy was standing in the corner, pointing his finger and laughing at me. And I had to admit, he had achieved a small victory over me. My voice, my identity, and my worship felt stolen. I knew my identity wasn't wrapped up in what I did, but in that moment I felt very empty and defeated.

I had to hold onto hope during the rocky start to our move. God called us to Redding, but it was a grueling transition. I kept hidden in my heart that my story wasn't over yet. I knew that at some point I'd either get a new guitar or have an opportunity to lead worship again. My small, personal victory was when I could remember that the loss didn't define me. My identity did not lie in what I did or didn't do. My identity was deep within me – that I was a child of God, rooted and grounded in Jesus. I was a daughter of the Most High King. That's what I held onto.

My guitars sat in the music room, broken and unused for a year and a half. Between the cost of the move, opening up a new store location, and many financial challenges, it just wasn't in the cards to fix or replace them. I kept praying that God would make a way, somehow. I couldn't let them go and just purchase a new guitar because of the irreplaceable memories and moments they represented between myself and Jesus.

I kept my spirits high. I may not have been leading others in worship, but I worshiped my heart out at our new church home and in my car or in the secret place. About a year and a half later, a gift was presented to me. Someone close to me offered to have them repaired, totally free of charge. I could not believe it. I didn't feel like I was deserving of this! I cried happy tears. Feelings of joy, gratitude, and humility filled my heart. I was reminded once again, that our God in Heaven cares about the deepest desires of our hearts, big or small. He is so good. He is so faithful.

 **Chapter 13**

POP-UP FLOP

"Celebrate your successes. Find some humor in your failures."

—Sam Walton

SEVERE TURBULENCE

When we moved to California, we had no intention of pausing the momentum with NHiM. From the outside looking in, it probably seemed abrupt and too soon to leave the Colorado store. Knowing it was important to leave it in good hands, we hired Matt's sister as our manager and added staff to keep the store thriving. Coincidentally, we left Colorado exactly three years to the day from when we opened the first NHiM location. A lot had happened in such a short amount of time. We hoped to be back often to check in on the store and the staff and make any necessary improvements.

We wanted to keep growing the brand. Now that we were in California, it was a good time to expand. Redding seemed like a great place to open up a pop-up or trial store. We chose a prime location, in a high-traffic area right in the center of town. We were near the main intersection of I-5 and 44, on the corner of Dana Drive and Hilltop Drive. We negotiated a six-month temporary lease and got started on a store buildout. Since this was a trial, we wouldn't invest too heavily on permanent store structures, but even with temporary builds it was still a large price tag.

We did much of the work ourselves, leveraging the architectural blueprints from the Colorado store. We were excited to work with the same custom woodwork company out of Denver to build our Scandinavian-inspired, pine pegboard walls and give this second store that same airy, modern, open layout. We worked our tails off, tirelessly and with little sleep, and were open within a little over a month of moving! It was completed in record time compared to our previous store builds.

It wasn't easy. We barely had time to get settled into our new home or get our kids acquainted with their new school due to the enormity of the work ahead of us. Besides the buildout, we needed to develop an inventory strategy, locally source and print graphic tees and sweatshirts, add women's fashion pieces, and carry new accessories. It was no small feat. Plus, we still had to continue marketing and sending email campaigns for our Colorado store, manage our staff from afar,

POP-UP FLOP

and advertise the new location prior to the Grand Opening.

Because we had no family in town and didn't have many friends yet, we had to roll with some less-than-ideal situations for our family. Our kids were with us at the store after school most days until opening day. The night before we opened, our three young girls were trying to sleep on chairs or on the floor, while we scurried around the store like headless-chickens until about three a.m. (yes, on a school night). Our middle daughter, Jewel, was glued to the TV watching cartoons until we made her try to lay down to get some sleep. Even still, we got it all done. We finished setting up the store and opened our 913 Dana Drive location, sandwiched between Jamba Juice and Mod Pizza, on Friday, October 19, 2018—just four and a half weeks after we arrived in California.

I remembered the thrill of opening day back in Colorado just two years earlier, when we could look out our glass windows to see a long line forming outside our spacious, 3,500-square-foot store. After adding the final touches, checking the iPads and receipt printers, and praying with our amazing staff, we were blown away and humbled by the local support and newcomers that showed up to our grand opening at Park Meadows Mall.

With this not-too-distant-memory in our back pocket, I had high hopes for a similar experience in Redding. At 10 a.m., we had tons of balloons, a DJ, and a big staff ready to greet the expected line of incoming supporters, welcoming us to their new town. But when we opened the doors, there was no line. The excitement and expectation we were experiencing inside the store was nowhere to be found on the outside. We pushed past the initial disappointment and kept our spirits up. Maybe it was wishful thinking, but we said to our team, "They'll come, I'm sure. Maybe no one shops this early in Redding." (Keep in mind, I tend to be overly optimistic, sometimes to a fault.)

As the day went on, a few individuals and passersby popped into the store here and there. We even met a nice homeless person who came in to use the phone. We rang up a handful of transactions and had the opportunity to pray with buyers, but it definitely wasn't the grand opening we'd imagined. The weekend got slightly busier, but we never saw the initial grandeur or reception we had hoped for in this second store location. Maybe the town was still dealing with the aftermath of loss due to the massive destruction of the 2018 Carr Fire in Shasta County. The timing of our store opening was probably not ideal, with expendable income at a low for many of the locals.

Regardless, we kept on. We spent Facebook (Meta) marketing money, created flyers to pass around town, told everyone we met about the store, and partnered with local businesses and churches in hopes of more people finding out about NHiM. We also experienced the dichotomy of the locals, who either loved or hated Bethel churchgoers. We started getting comments on our Facebook ads, with curses from people 'trolling' our social media saying they 'hoped our business fails' and even declaring harm upon our family. It was pretty disturbing, honestly, but this wasn't a fight against flesh and blood.

This was spiritual warfare. The darkness did not want our personal influence for the Kingdom of God or breakthrough in public prayer over this town. After all, we aimed to be a house of prayer that just looked like a clothing store. The opportunity to impact and pray for anyone who walked in, churched or unchurched, believing God for a miracle in their lives, held no price tag. The prince of this world knew this. So we kept praying and fighting to stay in business and to keep blazing a trail.

Besides, isn't it just like the enemy to cause you to doubt God's plans and intentions for your life? The lies he sends your way make you feel dumb, defeated, and unsure if you ever heard God in the first place. Yet God is always there to speak truth over us. That's the purpose of the secret place with Him. In prayer, in His presence, and in the Word, God makes crooked things straight. He takes the lies we've been listening to and throws them in the trash. That is why we need God every day. We have to renew our minds daily to rediscover who He is and who we are in Him (NHiM). To understand that God sees and knows us more than even we know ourselves. He knows the greatness He has placed within us and the incredible destination ahead, if we just *keep on keeping on.*

Christmas Troubles

We remained steadfast in our pursuit to build NHiM into the framework of this new town. We've always had a determination to do everything it takes to make it go. But two months following the opening, about a week before Christmas—just as holiday sales were about to spike so we'd hopefully get a return on all the capital we'd invested—we were hit with a literal storm.

Our store manager, Amy, was working that Sunday while our family was on a day trip in Sacramento. It had been raining pretty hard that day in Redding, but it didn't seem like anything to be concerned about. What we didn't know was that the egress of the drain pipe for all of the connected stores was directly above our store roof—and apparently, there were some holes and ceiling tiles near this drain that needed to be repaired. All of this became very evident when the heavy rain hit, because within a couple hours of the storm in Redding, it began *raining* in our store.

Amy called us with hesitation in her voice, letting us know that her husband had swung by the store to help her try to manage all the leaks. He was placing buckets everywhere he could, but it was getting worse by the minute. She said the ceiling tiles looked like a soggy wet diaper, about to burst. We got to the store as quickly as possible, panicking during the two-hour drive that felt like an eternity. Over the course of the day, the non-stop rain had permeated the roof leaks and our store was now completely flooded.

Walking into the store was like walking into a nightmare. We were in shock and disbelief as we looked around. Wet, crumbled ceiling tiles were all over our clothing and newly installed wood floor and display fixtures. Some of the wood fixtures were warped from water damage. The bigger loss was that almost half of our products and clothing items were damaged and no longer sellable. They were completely ruined. I felt such a lump in my throat.

It was rough, but God gave us an opportunity to work on our

character. We could choose joy or we could choose anger. There's always a silver lining if we choose to look up. The joy that we chose to focus on was that our team and so many friends quickly came to help as they heard the news. They showed up to the store and helped us move everything out, cleaned up the mess and water damage, and even assisted in moving back anything salvageable. The landlord fixed the leaks that week and we were back in business with the remaining clothing and displays.

The loss didn't put an end to everything. It didn't define the future of NHiM. It was just a roadblock of temporary loss and disappointment. God never said following Him would be easy. There are so many verses about this very thing. John 16:33 says, "I have told you these things, so that in me you may have peace. In this world you will have trouble. But take heart! I have overcome the world."

So what do we do in those moments? *Worship*. It's so counterintuitive to what feels right in the moment, but honestly the best thing you can do is to worship Jesus when things are rough. Romans 5:3-5 says, "We can rejoice, too, when we run into problems and trials, for we know that they help us develop endurance. And endurance develops strength of character, and character strengthens our confident hope of salvation. And this hope will not lead to disappointment. For we know how dearly God loves us, because he has given us the Holy Spirit to fill our hearts with his love."

Even when things go wrong and you question if God is still there, He will help you pick up the pieces and start walking again. Facts are facts. The Redding store was only open for six months. We invested much more than we ever made back. The low sales couldn't sustain the cost to remain open. The day we closed our doors was definitely disheartening. But God, in his Great mercy, still used that season to bring new opportunities and open new doors. Because this store failure—this short-lived 'pop-up-flop'—led us to our next adventure in Redding.

POP-UP FLOP

 **Chapter 14**

CRASH COURSE IN SCREEN PRINTING

"For every failure, there's an alternative course of action. You just have to find it. When you come to a roadblock, take a detour."

—Mary Kay Ash

SEVERE TURBULENCE

The day we closed up shop in Redding was rough. It didn't define us, but it still hurt. We tried to recoup any expenses we could, sending the remaining inventory to our Colorado store or selling it online, though online sales were an extremely small fraction of our business then. We took the pine pegboard walls and clothing displays with us, and even removed the wood floors we had installed to sell them.

As we locked up the doors for the last time, the buyer for the flooring came and was loading the floor planks into the back of his SUV. We had loaded up the NHiM trailer with the remaining walls and were about to leave the parking lot. We had sold the flooring for just about $1,000 (which was a steal for the buyer). His Mercedes SUV was parked right next to our Yukon and trailer. Out of nowhere, he opened his door while we pulled out. The door collided with the trailer, bent his door backwards, and put a long, deep dent in our no-longer-pristine NHiM trailer. Any profit from the floors would now go to an insurance claim. Ouch.

On a positive note, something new was coming. During the Christmas season, working with screen printers had a special set of challenges. When an item began to sell out due to popularity, we had to wait two weeks or more to get a restock from the printer. Then we had to ship it to the Colorado store, which was another weeklong delay. Sometimes we had issues with the print quality or loss of merchandise, plus the margins were not great. All of this got us thinking.

We'd been designing all of our garments and working very closely with the local screen printer, but hadn't delved into this industry on our own. We wanted to control the quality, lead time, placement of graphics, and cost. We'd learned a lot about the process and felt it was time to bring it in house. So we purchased a Riley Hopkins manual five-headed machine and basic dryer, and got started. We (and by "we," I mean Matt) took a crash-course in screen printing and learned as much as possible. We had also made a new friend (again named Jesus) with previous screen printing experience who helped us get started. He taught us everything he knew and helped us begin printing our

CRASH COURSE IN SCREEN PRINTING

clothing in-house.

We set up shop on our home property. Our 1,200-square-foot enclosed garage was a great starting location—minus the hot Redding summers without A/C and incoming dust from the gravel driveway. It was even technically rent-free, other than increased utility usage from the dryer. It was a great way to start screen printing with little upfront costs. By now, it was evident how important it was to not invest too heavily upfront in something unproven. It was fun when occasionally one of our goats would wander into the shop to say hello or stop by for a model shoot. (Kidding on the model shoot, but we did snap a few pics of them for Instagram.)

We began producing all our own garments, with many learning curves and challenges to overcome on the fly. Sometimes the ink didn't cure right, or the design was crooked, or the dryer was too hot and burned the garment. But we began to dial it in. There was also a promising new business relationship that had begun before we closed the Redding store with Bethel Media (which at the time was combined with Bethel Music). We had told them we were now screen printing for our brand, and they wanted us to produce their next product line for their Open Heavens Conference.

This new business relationship sent us full time into this secondary business venture. This was no longer a side hustle. We became NHiM Apparel & Manufacturing for the next season.

For our first client-project with Bethel Media, we took on a 1,500-piece project. Yes, you read that right: 1,500 pieces! It was just like us to jump into something new headfirst. Most people would start with printing 25 shirts or something, but nah, not us. When the blank garments arrived at our ranch, the pallets stacked high and filled an entire two-car garage! This project had shirts with six colors, four print locations, and some custom heat-applied felt application thrown in, which was also new for us. This was *no small project*. Looking back, we laugh now at the sheer labor of printing that many shirts on a manual press, but we didn't have the foreknowledge to know how difficult it would be.

111

SEVERE TURBULENCE

Thankfully, we had a lead time of six weeks to complete it. We spent a lot of late nights printing, folding, tagging, and bagging all the garments. Miraculously, we finished it. I can confidently say that we did a stellar job and they were so pleased with the results. It boosted our confidence to know we could not only supply our own printing needs for NHiM, but take on projects for new clients as well. After the financial loss of the Redding store, screen printing became a real blessing to be able to reduce costs, improve margins, and acquire a new type of sales. The Lord was stretching us, giving us a runway for continued growth.

CRASH COURSE IN SCREEN PRINTING

 **Chapter 15**

YOU WANT TO FIGHT?!

"In the confrontation between the stream and the rock, the stream always wins, not through strength but by perseverance."

—H. Jackson Brown

SEVERE TURBULENCE

HiM Apparel was now five years old. We'd made it through the infancy and toddler stages of the brand and pushed past a lot of challenges and setbacks. The Colorado store was still alive and thriving, though it definitely had its ups and downs in profit and loss. It had only been about one year since our move from Colorado to the small, rural town of Redding. Besides spiritual growth, part of the draw to move was that living in California was always a dream of ours. We never liked cold weather, and the idea of a warm climate with lakes or the opportunity for a short day trip to the beach seemed epic.

The manufacturing side of things was growing. We were doing all we could to make things work, but didn't yet know what would come from this move. We originally thought it would be for the new store in sunny California, because how cool would that have been? After being there for a year, we could see how the general clothing style in the town leaned towards urban western wear or thrifted clothing and less towards the street or city fashion of our brand. We also learned that stores like Walmart, Tractor Supply, and the local feed store were the most popular places to shop. Our shop in Redding just didn't fit.

Even with the new screen printing sales, we were still catching up to the aftermath of the financial loss. Month after month, bills overwhelmed us. The debt from the Redding store closure still hung over our shoulders. Even though sales were decent in Colorado, the huge costs to finish out the temporary and permanent store never paid themselves back. We had close to $250,000 in debt and didn't know how to escape it. Without business mentors or investors, we had no one to lean on for advice on how to make the business profitable or gain capital to pay for the large start-up costs we'd incurred. Bills continued to add up and the ability to pay for them all became next to impossible.

Not long after the closure of the Redding store, Matt came back into the house from the shop, overworked and overstressed, still working hard to keep everything running. He'd hit a realization that we could no longer pay the Colorado store rent, payroll, and other important debts due to a stream of lower sales and too many interest-only payments.

He came into our bedroom, anxious and weighed down. In a tense voice, he confessed, "Diane, come tomorrow, we can't make payroll or rent. I don't know what to do. We've done all of this for God, but I keep feeling like He's forgotten about us. Doesn't He know we're going to fail?!" I tried my best to fight back the tears from the news, knowing I needed to be strong for Matt at this moment. Through 15 years of marriage, we'd learned it wasn't good for both of us to be defeated. At least one of us needed to be strong to build up and encourage the other, even when we weren't in the mood to do so. Nothing good would come from both of us falling apart.

I told him to go out to the barn and just talk to Jesus. If you're wondering why the barn… that's where Matt found peace. He's always found joy in caring for animals. Besides, you couldn't stay upset for long looking at those adorable and comedic goats. He headed outside and kind of had it out with God. He was pretty upset that everything was about to fail, once again. It wasn't the first time we were on the brink of bankruptcy.

It's best to hear this part from Matt's point of view.

Matt:

Yeah, I was mad at God. How could he do this to us? Didn't he want us to spread His name through our brand? Didn't he want us to be able to pay our bills? Diane told me to calm down or go outside to the barn and vent. And so I did. And man, was it a real one. I yelled at the top of my lungs, asking God "Why?" I had given my everything to make His name known. "Why aren't You helping?" I yelled. I even asked Him if He wanted to fight! "Come down, Lord, let's go at it!" Man, was that stupid. Then it happened. Like a ton of bricks, the Lord hit me back with a command. "Go and read the story of Jacob and the Angel," He told me. And so I did. It reads:

SEVERE TURBULENCE

"During the night Jacob got up and took his two wives, his two servant wives, and his eleven sons and crossed the Jabbok River with them. After taking them to the other side, he sent over all his possessions.

This left Jacob all alone in the camp, and a man came and wrestled with him until the dawn began to break. When the man saw that he would not win the match, he touched Jacob's hip and wrenched it out of its socket. Then the man said, "Let me go, for the dawn is breaking!"

But Jacob said, "I will not let you go unless you bless me."

"What is your name?" the man asked.

He replied, "Jacob."

"Your name will no longer be Jacob," the man told him. "From now on you will be called Israel, because you have fought with God and with men and have won."

(Genesis 32: 22-28)

It was then that God confirmed to me to not let go until He blessed me. He revealed to me that I was a fighter like Jacob, refusing to give up or give in—striving with all that I had to make things work. But God reminded me of this. You see, Jacob had relied solely on his own merit to get things done, even if it meant deceiving others. Jacob's name means "heel grabber or trickster." But God changed it at that moment to Israel, which means "strives with God." This was a special moment for me with God. I needed a reminder to stop being so self-reliant (always stressing over the numbers in the bank account) and to instead strive with God. To not merely focus on what I could see in the natural, but rather keep my gaze on Him and expect the supernatural.

That night, Matt and I prayed and surrendered everything over to the Lord, knowing that we had to give all of our fears and worries to Him. We surrendered our business to Him too, asking Him to just take it if it didn't please Him anymore. Emotionally exhausted, we hit the pillow and went to bed.

The very next morning, God blessed us. We received the largest wholesale order to date from a mega church in Arizona. They wanted to carry NHiM in all of their bookstores. That paid for most of our pressing bills and allowed us to keep going.

The wholesale order was completely unexpected. It was a miracle. We could feel God's favor and love so tangibly. It showed us yet again the power of surrender. It pleases God greatly when we give Him control over every area of our lives, especially in our finances. He was showing us He hadn't gone anywhere; He hadn't forgotten about us. When we were ready to throw in the cards and be done, He told us to hold on until He blessed us. The bank account didn't have the final say—He did.

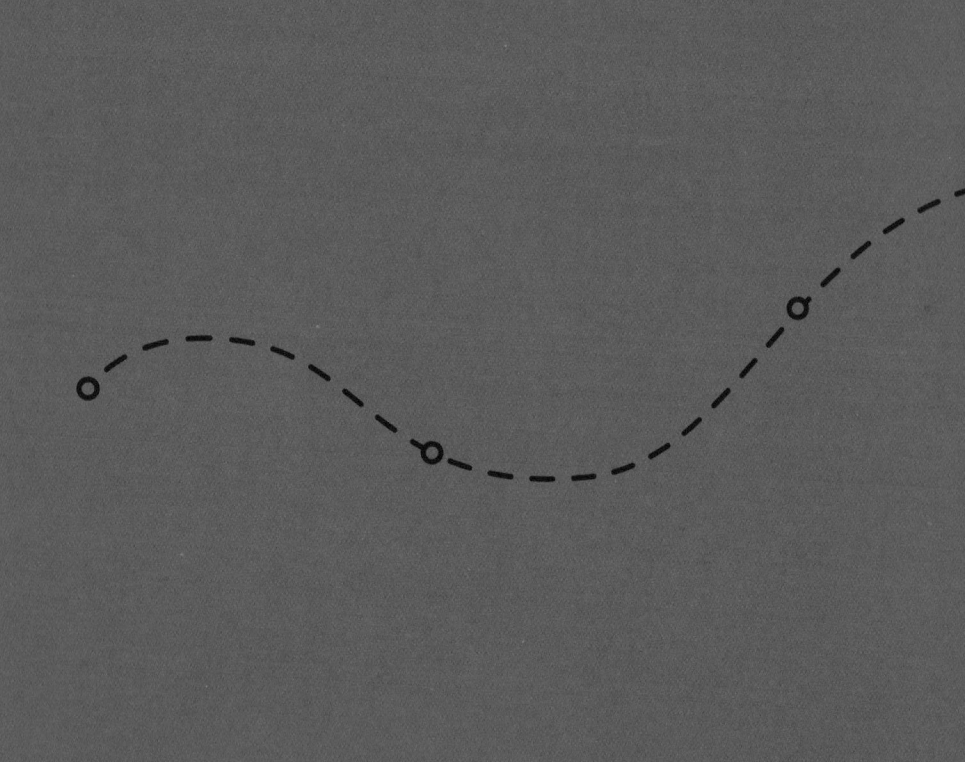

Part Four

RESUMING THE CLIMB

Starting our screen printing business venture — and letting go of it — taught us an important lesson. I had never wanted to be a screen printer. In fact, it was the last thing on my mind! I wanted to be a brand and a ministry, not a brand and a screen printer. Not only was it a lot of hard work, it was a tedious art to conquer, usually requiring years of trial and error. It felt like the identity and vision of NHiM was being challenged.

It would have been easy for us to become distracted with the money we were making from screen printing. But ultimately, we had to make another choice and recognize that building a screen printing empire wasn't our dream or a call on our lives. The Lord was giving us a key to open one door so we could get to the next door that needed to be unlocked.

Sometimes a blessing is temporary and only meant for a season. If you hold onto this temporary blessing too long, it becomes an idol and a distraction that will deter you from your destination. In moments of doubt, pray and lean into God's voice for direction. Stay fixated on the flight plan and be unwilling to deviate. Challenge every new "opportunity" that comes your way to see if it aligns with God's best for you. Not every good thing is a good thing.

— Matt

Chapter 16

ANGELS ARE REAL

"Miracles are a retelling in small letters of the very same story which is written across the whole world in letters too large for some of us to see."

—C.S. Lewis

SEVERE TURBULENCE

Things were starting to pick back up again for NHiM. New business was streaming in from screen printing and wholesale orders, and the brand was gaining more popularity. We had to learn to juggle a lot of roles. We didn't have enough excess cash flow to hire staffing to cover every role within the company, which meant Matt and I would carry the bulk of responsibilities. We had two people helping Matt with screen printing in our small shop, a full retail staff for the Colorado store, and one part-time employee helping fulfill the small, steady stream of online sales. The rest of the tasks were covered by Matt or myself.

From the very beginning, we were learning how to negotiate commercial lease agreements, graphic design, interior store design and merchandising, email marketing and online ads, learning what sells and what doesn't, growing a brand through social media, photography of the clothing, bookkeeping, sales strategies, management, and more. Whatever it was, we educated ourselves the best we could and found a way to accomplish it.

At the time, some of my main roles were photography, social media, marketing, email campaigns, website management, and creating the visuals or signage for the physical store. On certain days, I'd set up lifestyle model shoots or curate product-only photography for the website. On one particular day, I was overwhelmed by the to-do list, feeling underqualified and lacking creativity. In all honesty, I was getting fed up with the process. Matt suggested I retake the photos or work on the edit, which was probably necessary but not what I wanted to hear after feeling mentally defeated. Even though we have always been partners in building this business, it doesn't mean we always see eye to eye. We're different people who have different opinions and ideas for things.

Later that night, what started as a conversation about photography became a heated discussion. Even though we juggled the many responsibilities of the brand, it didn't always mean we enjoyed those tasks or thrived in them. I was ready to find someone more talented than myself to capture the vision we had in mind, but the finances weren't there. In the swirl of frustrations, this heated discussion grew into a big argument after we tucked our kids into bed. About halfway through it all, we barely knew what we were fighting about anymore. At that point, it was all about winning the fight.

We were so lost in the argument that we didn't even think about how loud our voices were or that our children were upstairs trying to sleep. A couple days later, our daughter Bella shared something that had happened that night. She told us that she was lying in her bed, crying her eyes out to Jesus, asking Him to help. She needed comfort and wanted to know everything would be okay with her mom and dad. She already knew He was a loving God, but she needed to feel loved in a real way in that moment because she was scared.

As she was praying and talking to Jesus, *an angel appeared in her room.* The angel perched on the dresser next to Bella's bed, filing her nails. (Try not to write the story off just yet). Bella described the angel as a beautiful female with dark skin, long black curly hair, and gold wings that reflected different colors of the rainbow. She had a choker necklace with a music note on it, which Bella believed symbolized that the angel played an instrument in Heaven.

Bella sat up in her bed in awe, feeling an instant connection with the angel. Instead of being scared, she felt peace and comfort fill her room. She then looked outside her window and saw another, much larger angel standing outside her deck and window. It was an angel of protection, and it was spreading its wings and arms over our home. Bella began to talk with the mysterious angel on her dresser. She didn't have to communicate verbally; they could somehow understand each other without words, in the spirit.

Bella asked the angel what she was doing. She said she was painting her nails. Bella asked her what color, and the angel told her it was the name of a color we didn't have here on Earth, but it was the color of Heaven. They exchanged words for a while longer and Bella asked her if her mom and dad would be okay. The angel (whom God revealed to Bella was her guardian angel) told her that everything would be okay. She said God was protecting our home and family. Bella fell asleep and rested peacefully through the night.

Being completely honest, Bella's story was a little hard to believe at first. Though I believed in angels and read their stories in the Bible, I had never experienced anything like that personally. Plus, I figured the angel wouldn't be quite that cool or modern. But as Matt and I chatted, we realized that it wasn't Bella's style to make up stories. She's the firstborn and has always been a responsible, mature, "rule-follower" type. Her experience with the angel encouraged us. The idea that angels were surrounding and protecting our home was very reassuring.

We continued to pray and ask God about this divine encounter. What we began to discover was that God encounters us in the ways that meet our needs personally. And angels can come in all shapes and sizes, as the Bible describes them. God knew what would speak most to Bella. He knew what she would relate to. God cares about all those details. The angel was so beautiful and fashionable in Bella's eyes. What a personal God we serve. After this encounter, Bella's eyes became more opened to the spiritual realm. This was new to our family. Over the coming months, she began to meet and see each of our guardian angels and learn their names. She would see them around our property, as she was just going about her day or playing with the animals. They each were so unique and different, which was amazing. They'd walk about and circle the property, watching over us. Bella still sees into the angelic realm today.

Running a business with your spouse is hard on the marriage. That's not to say it can't or shouldn't be done, but it pulls and prods you in the most challenging ways. Matt and I had to learn how to speak life into each other, even when we're tired. We've had to learn how to have grace for each other's shortcomings. It's been one of the hardest things, but also has grown our marriage the most. Learning how to not let the business take over your family life, even when you work out of your home, is hard.

That's where creating healthy boundaries within the home and marriage is helpful. Learn when to clock in and clock out. And most of all, learn to love God and put Him first. It makes everything else fall into place. If other tasks and to-do's take precedence over our time with Jesus, usually it all falls apart. But learning to balance it all with God's wisdom will help everything else come into alignment.

I wasn't thankful Matt and I had the argument that night, but I'm thankful we serve a God who makes beautiful things out of our messes. He used the experience to show us that He is working behind the scenes, in the places we can't physically see. The fact that He so tenderly blessed our daughter during this moment reminds us that our God sees and cares for every one of us—especially the littlest ones.

Chapter 17

GOLD DUST & SOARING SALES

"All you need is faith, trust, and a little bit of ~~pixie~~ **gold** dust."

—Paraphrased from Peter Pan

SEVERE TURBULENCE

As January 2020 rolled around, news of COVID-19 outbreaks loomed. We'd just wrapped up 2019 with a great Christmas season. We were full of vision for the new year and ready to continue building momentum. And yet, we had no idea what season lay ahead, or what the entire world was about to experience all together. By mid-March, COVID was in full swing and the nation was entering lockdown. Retailers everywhere were required to close their operations in Colorado, including inside the mall. The only exception to closing was to provide curbside pickup or delivery if you had an exterior-facing entrance. Our store was interior-facing with no external door.

The news of this hit hard. It had already been a slow sales start for 2020, due to the debilitating fear the world was experiencing. No one wanted to leave their homes with the notion that they could be personally infected by this new virus. Yet for us, our survival as a brand required continued sales.

Matt has always worked well under pressure, so he was brilliant and quick to respond to the extenuating circumstances. He applied early to the Federal grants and forgiveness loans. He made sure to look for all available governmental help for small businesses, which was what we needed. We received a couple of grants to keep our Colorado staff employed and pay for some overhead expenses. Though sales remained very low with the only incoming sales happening online, we were able to provide employment for our staff during those couple of months during the closure. But instead of having them just sit at home with nothing to do, we created an online chat with live prayer for our customers. We also had a 1-800 phone number to call into for prayer. Our staff was able to work from home, pray with customers, or help answer any questions. This chat option was a new bonus feature for our website as well.

The unknown part of the equation going into this was our sales. We had previously received the majority of our NHiM sales in store, not online. Though we had a good website, we hadn't learned to successfully market our ecommerce store in a way that would result in

GOLD DUST & SOARING SALES

sufficient sales. 90% of all of our sales were in store, with only 10% or less coming in online. So we couldn't just fall back on the website for customer retention and sales.

There was no way to explain what came next other than God's divine hand of intervention. We were about to experience another marking moment that would result in a miracle.

One afternoon, as we were preparing for the temporary closure of our store location, Matt pulled me into the detached garage on our property to speak with me privately. He couldn't seem to shake off his worry. We were already behind on bills with the slow first quarter, plus now there was a total pause of incoming screen printing jobs due to churches and clients not needing new merch. Conferences and concerts were being canceled due to COVID. Money was not coming in at the speed that the bills were. It wasn't looking good. With the switch to purely online, how would we sustain this? Of course we could use the grant money for a little while to keep our staff on payroll and cover basic rent expenses for our store, but there were still loans to pay, restock of inventory to purchase, and other expenses that we needed the influx of sales to cover.

Matt shared openly with me about his real concerns and the thoughts plaguing him. He was saying things like, "Maybe God doesn't actually care about our business or its success. Does it really matter to Him? I don't think He cares about our sales or that we started this for Him. Maybe what we've done hasn't even made a difference in people's lives." And the list of defeating statements went on.

We've all had moments when crippling fear felt overwhelming, or when doubts about God's love for us felt all too convincing, making us wonder if God even cares about the details or needs of our lives. We know that in theory He does, but can't understand at the time why we aren't seeing or experiencing it. It's another one of those 'character-building' opportunities. Another chance to show our real commitment to the King of Kings when things aren't going well.

Back-track with me to something that happened about a week before this. It was a Sunday afternoon. Non-essential businesses were on lockdown (including churches), so church consisted of online viewing. We were glad to still hear the worship and message, but it wasn't the same as going in person. We wanted a change of scenery that day, so we decided to grab a coffee at one of our favorite spots, Theory Coffee, and then watch church online in our car with the family.

We happened to run into the Senior Pastor of Bethel Church, Bill Johnson, in the coffee shop after placing our order. We hadn't seen him much outside of church, so it was nice to say hello. They had already filmed the church service, so apparently there was no need for him to be at the building. We said hello and he greeted us back with such warmth and kindness. Regardless of naysayers (as there always are when you've built a massive movement and church organization), Pastor Bill is truly the same person outside of church that he is on the platform. He carries the presence of God and a peace over his life that is evident. We conversed for a minute, and then went back to our car to 'watch church.'

When we got home that afternoon, there was a mysterious excitement within us. I actually felt something like electricity shooting throughout my body. Whether it was church, the message, or the time of worship, something had shifted in each of us. The Holy Spirit was moving strongly and in a new way within us and drawing us closer.

We had just walked in the door when Bella asked if we could open up the hatch to the attic. There was a cut-out in the ceiling that you could remove in one of our downstairs bathrooms to access the attic. For whatever reason, we'd never opened it to look inside during the two years we'd lived there. She was curious if there was anything left in there from the previous owners. We said yes, of course, and Matt grabbed a ladder from the garage and removed the attic door. Bella asked if she could be the first to look in.

She peeked into the small, dark corner of the tiny attic and seemed surprised. She said, "It looks like Christmas decorations were stored up here or something. There's gold glitter everywhere!" Matt and I and the family proceeded to take our turns on the ladder and look in. We saw the same fine dusting of what looked like gold glitter all over the beams of the attic. Yet there were no signs of fake pine tree needles or ornaments.

For some reason, there was wonder in it all. It seemed that God was trying to tell us something. About a month or two earlier, I'd had a dream about our home holding hidden value or treasure, so the gold dust was even more intriguing. We and the kids decided to put on worship music and just pursue Him as a family. We were singing and worshiping freely in our living room. Some of our girls are dancers, so they were dancing in our living room as their expression of worship. I even got the boldness (since it was our own home) to move around more than usual as well!

All of a sudden, our kids noticed the wood beams on the ceiling of our lodge-like home were covered in what appeared to be the same gold glitter or dust that we had seen in the attic! What was going on?! The gold dust wasn't there before. I'd read stories about gold dust appearing and symbolizing the presence of God, but I didn't have the faith for it or the comprehension for it. Why would something like this happen to us? We thought maybe we were seeing things or that the wood just had a weird sap-substance on it.

Matt was totally baffled. He sat in the kitchen and started researching on his phone all the reasons why wood beams could have a golden glitter appearance. But everything he pulled up online that could occur naturally wasn't what we were seeing. It wasn't beads of sap or years of condensation expressing itself from the beams. As he was busy trying to explain away what we were seeing, the girls and I just kept worshiping and dancing! God was showing us something special.

Then one of our kids said, "Mom! Look at my hands and arms!" I looked to see that her hands and arms were covered in fine gold dust. It was like something you'd see in a gold makeup shimmer powder. I looked at my hands and saw it too! It was all over my arms and palms. All the kids had it. We hadn't touched the attic or beams, either, so it didn't make sense! Matt looked at his hands and it wasn't on him at all. We all laughed! It seemed like God was showing us that faith made it appear and though Matt typically had enormous levels of faith, at that moment he just couldn't believe this was supernatural or from God. Right then, it hit him. Like the rest of us, he knew this was only the Lord's doing.

Our littlest child, Eden, who was five years of age at the time, asked us all to sit down on the couch. It felt like she was the Sunday school teacher, ready to teach us. She said, "I think we all need to ask God what the gold dust means." So we sat and prayed and asked God, each on our own, what it meant. A couple of the kids spoke up and felt like it was God's love showing itself. In fact, all of our daughters said something similar to that effect. Matt and I had nothing. We just couldn't quite hear an answer or response as to why it appeared or what it meant.

Now, let's go back to the conversation with Matt in the shop, about a week later, when Matt was being vulnerable with me about his concerns. After he was done venting, I tried my best to encourage him. I didn't have all the right words because I knew there was some truth in his worries and valid questions that needed to be addressed. But I wanted so badly to bring hope to his heart and reassure him that I believed everything would work out. I reminded him that God always comes through for us and that I knew He would help us again.

He kept pacing back and forth from the house to the shop, trying to get some tasks accomplished for work. He was trying to keep his mind busy to avoid the uncertainty. Our youngest daughter, Eden, was swinging alone on the tree swing by the house. She asked him, each time he walked by, if he could push her on the swing. He wanted to, but his anxious mind was preventing him from taking a time out from his work, so he kept telling her, "Not right now, sweetie. Maybe later."

She was persistent, though. The third time she asked with a little more 'whine' in her tone, so he knew it was time to be a good father and just stop what he was doing to give her some of his time.

As he was pushing her on the swing, she asked him, "Daddy, did you ever ask God what the gold dust meant?"

He said, "I did, but I didn't really hear anything."

"Well I did, and He told me what it meant," Eden said.

GOLD DUST & SOARING SALES

Surprised by her remark, Matt asked, "Really? What did He say?"

Something switched right then. It was as if Eden was speaking with wisdom that wasn't her own. She began to tell Matt the following:

"Remember how much gold dust there was everywhere? Well, God told me that's how much He thinks about you. And do you remember how shiny it was? That's what He sees when He looks at you. God said that He cares about your business and your sales. He said that if you were to take the gold dust and stack it on top of each other, it would pile up to Heaven. He said that's how your sales will be and that's how many people you've impacted through your ministry. That's all, Daddy. Now can you keep pushing me on the swing?"

Matt almost fell over. He's not one to cry easily, but his eyes got watery. He knew God was speaking through her. Matt hastily asked if she could repeat what she said, so he could record it and keep it to remember. She tried, but the moment had already passed and she couldn't remember everything. It was like God, in His loving kindness, stooped down and countered Matt's every fear. Matt said it felt like a holy moment. God literally spoke to us in the most innocent, meaningful of ways – through our own child — and it was beautiful.

A couple weeks later, with this miracle sitting in our rearview mirror and the reality of the impending bills creeping up and taunting us again, a breakthrough began to emerge. The promised miracle of sales was beginning to unfold. Our physical store had just temporarily closed and our staff was home on standby to pray with or help any online shoppers. Our online store was barely active at this point, with about $100-150 in daily sales on average.

But one morning, shortly after the prophetic word from our daughter, our online sales started to shoot up. We use Shopify as our online sales platform, and we kept hearing the "cha-ching" sound it makes when someone completes a purchase on your site. By the end of the day, we'd surpassed $1,000 in sales—about 10x our usual performance! We could not believe it. Maybe it was a fluke, or maybe it was God. We weren't quite sure yet, but we were so incredibly thankful.

It kept happening, almost every day. We began to see greater traffic increases and sales than we'd typically had even in our physical store. We weren't doing any paid advertising at that point either, so it couldn't be because of our own efforts. One of our new products—a 'God is good' custom tie-dyed hoodie—started selling like wildfire. We had started with 100 pieces as a trial from our 'blanks' supplier in Los Angeles. Adjusting to the extraordinary sales, we turned around and ordered 300, then 500, then 1,000. We ended up selling over 2,000 of the hoodies in a very short window of time. For us, this was record-breaking.

It was very clear that this was God. There was no other explanation. The sales began to stack up and we were finally able to pay our bills. We even started to turn a small profit again. We eventually leaned into the world of online marketing on social platforms, which resulted in greater sales. Nothing could top the return on zero ad spend during that season, though. It was such a gift to be reminded that God is our Provider and money is not. That is one thing we've had to learn over the years. Yes, money might pay the bills, but God is the Creator of finances and of provision. Just look at what Jesus says in Matthew 6:26: "Look at the birds of the air; they do not sow or reap or store away in barns, and yet your heavenly Father feeds them. Are you not much more valuable than they?"

God's love and care for us—those made in His image—far exceeds any other product of his Creation. He reminds us all throughout His word that He cares so deeply for us and desires for us to pursue Him over money. And by worshiping Him alone, He will provide. It may not always be in the way we think or in the timing we expect, but He asks us to trust Him. God's actions and ways are above ours. We may not always understand why He does certain things, but we can rest assured that He is looking out for us, even in moments when gold dust appears.

GOLD DUST & SOARING SALES

 **Chapter 18**

WHEN GOD CLOSES ONE STORE...

"Every adversity, every failure, every heartache carries with it the seed of an equal or greater benefit."

—Napoleon Hill

SEVERE TURBULENCE

Online sales were still thriving, but so was COVID. When the mandates to close non-essential businesses had somewhat lifted, we were given the opportunity to reopen our doors at the mall. Due to the square footage and layout of our narrow store, we were only approved to have two customers and one employee in the store at any given time—with a requirement to remain six-feet apart. This would be a challenge. We typically had at least two people running the store and definitely more than two people shopping at a given time. How would we reach our sales minimums once we reopened? Or pay for all the overhead costs? Consumers were still nervous to leave their homes. Most people in the region were choosing to stay home until the spread of the disease slowed down.

With the extremely high monthly rent (you don't want to know the dollar amount), it didn't make sense to reopen yet. These were unchartered waters. We didn't know how to handle this new reality. We looked for advice from friends, family, and business leaders. Most of all, we prayed. Ultimately, the decision was ours to make. Besides, nobody wanted to tell us what we didn't want to hear. No one felt comfortable telling us that maybe it was time to shut our doors for good. That was too weighty and nauseating.

We had invested countless hours and dollars into building a store and brand presence in the community. We had a lot of local support. The NHiM store had a homegrown, Colorado feel that many people were proud to be a part of from the beginning. They had helped us grow this from the ground up—from setting up at concerts, to opening a kiosk in the mall, to sustaining a store and an online marketplace.

We had been in the mall for five years. We regularly held Bible studies in the store with our staff, prayed for countless people, witnessed real-life miracles, and felt honored to represent Jesus in the mall. Though we had moved away from Colorado two years prior, the store was a literal *child* to us, and we grieved the thought of losing it and no longer having any physical roots left in Colorado. We still loved the community, the people, and the heart behind our decision to be in the mall in the first place. We didn't want to lose our marketplace-ministry efforts.

After much prayer, we found peace. With no promise of how quickly the market or economy would bounce back, it felt like the right time to see if we could break our lease. We had to try to relieve ourselves of the pressure to perform in sales. Even though we had finally made a decision, a new reality hit us. What if the mall said no and wouldn't let us out of our lease? We still had two more years remaining, and the leasing company strictly enforced its lease agreements. Nervously, we sent an email with a letter of intent requesting to break our agreement. We prayed anxiously for God to intervene in the situation and make a way out for us.

We received an email back from the leasing team with the answer we'd hoped for. They said our lease could be terminated early! However, the penalty was that they'd keep our security deposit. $34,000 was a lot of money to lose. In addition, we'd need to leave our custom wall fixtures and any improvements we'd made to the space. Another blow. Stricken with further financial loss, we still felt peace on the decision and decided to move forward.

We shared the bittersweet news with our staff, which meant they would need to look for new employment. We genuinely didn't want anyone to be without a job. We prayed for our staff to find provision going forward and we kept them on payroll as long as we were able. On July 8, 2020, we closed our doors for good. We began to liquidate any free-standing furniture or fixtures on Facebook Marketplace, and our staff worked hard to package up all inventory and ship it to our home in California. We'd be fulfilling all online orders out of Northern California from that point on.

Though we had peace and hope for the future, a little piece of us died that day when the store closed. Even though we were gaining newfound online sales, we still were sad to lose what we'd built. We went through all the stages of grief. For any of you who have owned a business and had to close its doors, you can understand the roller coaster of emotions I'm referring to. It's painful. It's a loss that's hard to put into words. It was another opportunity for us to choose joy. To worship in the midst of the storm. None of it made sense, but we had to trust God once more.

A chapter may have been closing, but it wasn't the end of NHiM's story by any means. And honestly, we will forever be thankful for our experiences in Park Meadows Mall. Good things don't always last forever, and we have to be okay with that. We got to keep so many memories from our tenure there. I remember all the family and friends who helped us set up the store, the late nights putting up new inventory, and the mini concerts we held there. There was the time we were moving store locations and my mom hit her head on the glass door (yikes, sorry Mom) and the time floods of customers showed up to film their video testimonials. I remember pre-opening hours where we sang at the top of our lungs to worship music, and all the times we'd come into the store to see one of our staff members sharing the gospel or praying with a customer who was moved to tears. All of these are moments we treasure and won't ever forget.

In moments of loss, it's important we open our eyes and ears to what Jesus is saying. And it's healthy to go through all the stages of grief. I know beyond a shadow of a doubt that our God is good and that He cares about each and every one of His kids. He uses *everything* for His glory and for the good of those who love Him, who are called according to His purpose (Romans 8:28).

During this season, I tried an exercise to help me navigate the grief and loss. I took a piece of paper and made two columns. In one column, I wrote the things I'd lost and the hurt I was experiencing in detail. In the other column, I wrote out all the good things that came out of that season or what good might come. I even wrote out the small, insignificant details. And then I gave it to the Lord. I asked Him to take our hearts and mend them. To fill in all the cracks or crevices needing to be repaired. It never fails. He will turn sorrow into joy, mourning into dancing. I promise.

WHEN GOD CLOSES ONE STORE...

In the Bible, it says:
"to bestow on them a crown of beauty
    instead of ashes,
the oil of joy
    instead of mourning,
and a garment of praise
    instead of a spirit of despair.
They will be called oaks of righteousness,
    a planting of the Lord
    for the display of his splendor." (Isaiah 61:3)

New Vision for the Future

Following the close of the Colorado store, we poured ourselves into developing a better visual experience for our online store and further building our screen printing business. The shop at our home was getting crammed, so we found a great warehouse in Redding near the airport, with a fair price-per-square-foot and a short-term lease. After praying about it and feeling the Lord's peace on it, we decided to give it a try and moved in on August 14, 2020. We had to be as frugal as possible, so we invested in used equipment. Matt found a screen printing shop in the Bay Area that was closing their doors and liquidating their machines, ink, and supplies, and he locked in a great package deal. We made the leap to an automatic press with a large conveyor dryer. We built shelving to house our online inventory along with inventory for client projects.

  We hired a designer and photographer out of Atlanta to give our designs a fresh look and take our photography to the next level. And it worked. He knew how to relate to a broader market and give our brand an urban feel. With the new changes, we ended the year strong and had a great Christmas season. We were starting to reach a younger demographic. Prayer was still at the core of our mission, so we continued offering this for our online community. We also invested in two families who felt called to move from Colorado to California to support the vision of NHiM. They both had pastoral backgrounds and would help us with any immediate needs the company had. We invited them to live in 'community' with us on our property. Doing life together was special as they became dear friends, and these newly filled positions would help us to fulfill new roles as things grew busier.

The following February, an opportunity came that we couldn't pass up. We had the chance to manage the screen printing and fulfillment for a worship and recording artist on a non-stop tour. We were already growing as a local screen printing provider, but fulfillment was new to us. It meant we'd be shipping all of the artist's online orders and warehousing their goods. We'd also be managing inventory and shipping merchandise to every concert. It was another new business layer with a heavy workload.

We began working double shifts, families in tow. We'd be there until 10 p.m. some nights, printing, folding, bagging, and boxing in order to meet each deadline. Plus, we still had to squeeze in all NHiM restocking, fulfillment, and other client work. There were times the load was too heavy, but we sustained this new growth for about another year.

Through a turn of events, we decided the extra workload of providing screen printing and fulfillment for the recording artist was a major distraction from our brand, so we ended the agreement to work together. We paused on taking new clients and returned to focus solely on the NHiM brand. The screen printing business had become its own animal. Ultimately, we realized it wasn't the dream or call on our lives to build a screen printing empire, and there was freedom in that recognition. Knowing when to let go allowed us to fully embrace what we were truly meant to build.

WHEN GOD CLOSES ONE STORE...

 **Chapter 19**

RENT YOUR HOME OUT

"Jesus made a payment for the miracle you need."

—Bill Johnson

SEVERE TURBULENCE

We've always done our best to steward our finances within the business and pay off expenses, but there were many times we just couldn't make it happen on our own. Whether it was due to the ebb and flow of sales, the interest from loans, high overhead costs, the COVID effect, or starting the business from scratch with no investors, there were many times we ran out of money.

During one of those financially stressful times, Matt went to the warehouse to pick up the business mail. Looking through a stack of bills, he was surprised to come across an unexpected expense—we owed $10,000 and it was due immediately. We didn't have it. No amount of scrounging, scraping, or sales could get us that much money that fast. Not wanting to cause insecurity about company finances, Matt kept the news private and left the warehouse in a panic, then headed home to talk to me about possible solutions.

Over the next couple days, our anxiety grew. We couldn't come up with any ways to pay for this bill and needed a miracle. One afternoon that week, Matt was driving home with our youngest daughter, Eden, while I was picking up the other girls from after-school activities. As he turned onto our street, he stopped to check the mail. Our mailbox was an old-school, unlocked, personal mailbox right on a major highway. Technically, anyone could take our mail at any point in time. It definitely wasn't secure.

As he pulled out the mail, he noticed a yellow manila envelope with "Matt & Diane" written in large letters on the front. It was unaddressed and had no stamps on it, so it had clearly been hand-placed in the mailbox. He opened it and found another envelope inside it, with a reference to James 1:17, which says: "Every good and perfect gift is from above, coming down from the Father of the heavenly lights, who does not change like shifting shadows." He opened the envelope and found a wad of 100 dollar bills with the bank tag around it showing it amounted to $10,000!!!

What in the world?! Eden and Matt sat in the car in total shock. It was exactly the funds we needed to pay for the bill! We had no idea who gave it to us, or how anyone could have known we needed the money. It felt like God hand-delivered it himself. To this day, no one has ever revealed they were the giver. It was an incredible miracle and gift that we thanked God for.

Months later, we stepped out in faith again. It was our style to do whatever it took to create additional streams of income when the brand wasn't profitable enough. Various ministries had approached us with requests to use our lodge-style home and acreage for day-use and overnight events. So we began hosting youth camps, teacher retreats, college events, and more at our home. It got us thinking that maybe there was value in commercializing the use of our home and property.

One thing we've always tried to practice is to think and "dream" with God. We all have innate passions, ideas, and desires, but it's another thing to sit before God in prayer and ask Him for new ideas. When you take the time to really listen to God, He can speak into your heart about anything—from business ideas to ministry ideas, wisdom for life, strategies, and more. We're very accustomed to talking during prayer, but listening is just as important—if not more so. Having a pen and paper is helpful too, so you can jot down ideas and whispers that pop into your head. You might think it's just your brain, but if you're spending time with the Lord, it just may be Him speaking.

One of my all-time favorite verses comes from 1 Kings 19, where the Lord appears to Elijah on the mountain.

> "The Lord said, 'Go out and stand on the mountain in the presence of the Lord, for the Lord is about to pass by.' Then a great and powerful wind tore the mountains apart and shattered the rocks before the Lord, but the Lord was not in the wind. After the wind there was an earthquake, but the Lord was not in the earthquake. After the earthquake came a fire, but the Lord was not in the fire. And after the fire came a gentle whisper."

SEVERE TURBULENCE

God wasn't in the wind, He wasn't in the earthquake, and He wasn't in the fire, but He was in the whisper. I think that's so true for us today as well. There's so much noise around us, pulling us in many different directions, but usually God isn't the one shouting at us. If there's a lot of swirl and confusion, He's probably not in it. He is, however, in the quiet, whispering to our souls, waiting for us to be silent long enough to hear Him.

In one of those quiet times with the Lord, I heard a whisper to put our home on Airbnb. The only issue was, we were living in it! We had three kids, two dogs, and nearly 100 outdoor animals that needed our daily care and attention. I started getting an idea for a "farm stay" that would be attractive to people traveling from a couple hours away or from the San Francisco Bay Area, looking for a retreat. Between the open land, the outdoor pool, the sweet animals (think petting-zoo experience), and the roomy bedrooms that could sleep quite a few guests with some additional beds, we started to realize this could be a really great concept. But I also knew the competition was high, and the likelihood of being noticed on Airbnb or VRBO among all the options was slim.

Then I heard something wilder as I prayed. "Charge $1,000 per night." Huh?! I thought I was definitely crazy. No one would pay that kind of money to stay in a remote home, two-and-a-half hours from the Sacramento Airport. But Matt and I had peace on it. Matt said "Let's do it!" So I began staging the home to depersonalize the decor and feel more retreat-like. I added a couple beds in the large rooms and moved all personal items to the locked closets. We installed a secret door within our master bedroom closet that would allow the guest to use part of the closet for their clothes, with a locked door that hid the rest of our clothing behind it. I'm not going to lie: this new transition was tricky for our kids. It was hard on them to let go of the little personal things that made their room, their room. As a parent, that was hard to watch.

I took some basic photos of the home with my iPhone and listed it on Airbnb at $1,000 per night. Within days, we got our first booking!

RENT YOUR HOME OUT

We were blown away. It felt like a miracle. If this continued, this would help us subsidize our income whenever there was a downtrend in screen printing or online sales. It was truly an answer to prayer. We required a two-night minimum stay during the off-season, and a three- to four-night minimum stay during holidays. The only issue was, we needed somewhere to stay on the weekends or weekdays while it was booked out!

At first, we just booked a cheap hotel for our family for a couple nights and then returned back home to clean it and live in it again until the next booking. Yet that wasn't ideal as it was cutting into the profits. So we got creative. We spent the night in the NHiM warehouse with air mattresses. It was humbling. There was no shower or kitchen—just a microwave, refrigerator, sink, and toilet.

We needed a better solution if this were going to continue. We had two RV hookups on our property that would allow us to park an RV and live in it when the home was booked out, still allowing us to feed and care for the animals. We didn't want to necessarily embark on 'full-time RV living' with a family of five, but felt it could be a fun new adventure for a few nights or weekends here and there.

The home was consistently getting booked for eight to 15 nights per month, so we needed a better solution than the warehouse. It really wasn't a great time to invest in an RV, considering that the point of renting out our home was to help cover our bills. Yet we also felt a new prompting from the Lord to go on a mission trip as a family.

We had spent a lot of time laboring behind the scenes for the business, staying up until midnight, printing, shipping, quoting, and fulfilling orders. It was time to recalibrate our mission. Since closing the physical stores and becoming strictly an ecommerce company, we really desired a way to minister in person. We wanted to practice sharing the gospel as a family, listening to the leading of the Holy Spirit and obeying His word. We had a good amount of bookings and micro weddings already set for the upcoming summer and could easily choose to be gone for a month.

The time had come to embark on our first mission trip as a family.

SEVERE TURBULENCE

Our kids were 14, 12, and 9 and really loved Jesus. They were excited about the idea of going on a month-long mission trip on the coast of California. As we were praying about buying an RV, our good friends called us on FaceTime one Saturday morning and said, "We found your RV, and it's such a good deal! Hurry up and meet us here before someone else buys it!" So we jumped in the car and drove to the Best Buy parking lot and took it for a test drive. It was an older Class C RV, but had been kept in really good condition with low mileage. It was a small fraction of the cost of a new one and it would hold its value if we needed to resell at some point.

After a brief family meeting and prayer inside the potential new RV, we were given the green light by God. We walked around the RV and quietly dedicated it to the Lord. We asked God to help us pay it off easily and for the ability to use the vehicle for His glory. We asked Him to help us learn to do ministry as a family and to share His gospel through love. Once it was parked on our property, we had a couple months to adjust to living "small" as a family of five in this special RV before heading out on the road.

Renting out our home was inconvenient. It was untraditional and uncomfortable. It was awkward to explain to others why we were doing it. Friends and family couldn't imagine sharing their homes, beds, dishes, and possessions with random strangers. I agree, it seemed odd! It was also super challenging to take all of our food and groceries out of the kitchen and refrigerator every time we had a renter. Ugh, I do not miss that! Not everything is logical or easy to explain when it comes to ideas from God. But it really helped us to get through any tight times financially and not give up on our purpose.

Sometimes there are just things you need to do to provide for your family. What's important is leaning into God's voice and learning to trust His ways above ours.

RENT YOUR HOME OUT

 **Chapter 20**

TAKING IT TO THE STREETS

"Whatever we do, we must not treat the Great Commission like it's the Great Suggestion."

—Charles R. Swindoll

SEVERE TURBULENCE

With summer just a few weeks away, we were ready to embark on our RV mission trip. It wasn't going to be a conventional mission trip with a perfect itinerary. Our focus would be street evangelism and prayer, distribution of resources to those in poverty, partnering with other active ministries, and spreading God's hope and love to everyone we met. We were going to learn how to do life differently on the road as a family by actively listening to the Holy Spirit. Think of it as being on "high alert" from moment to moment – to practice being sensitive to the voice of God by praying and acting upon each decision.

We began to share the news, posting on our NHiM social platforms that a West Coast mission trip was coming up for our family. We asked for donations to be made on GoFundMe to help us purchase supplies to distribute. We would give away $10,000 of NHiM clothing to people we met on the trip as a tool to start a conversation about our faith and to help clothe those in need. We didn't map out our route or book any RV slots in advance, trusting God to give us daily direction. We told our kids that they had just as much ability to hear God's voice as we did, and that together, as a family, we would ask God to guide us on where to stay, where to stop, and whom to minister to.

Before leaving for the trip, we took a good look at the RV. We'd be spending a long time on the road and wanted to use every opportunity to share God's hope with the world. We worked with a friend to add giant decals to the exterior, incorporating our NHiM logo and "God is good" logos on each side of the motor home. We added QR codes that led to a video on our site, showing the work we were doing on the road.

As we headed out that July, we had anticipation in our hearts, eager for Him to be our guide. It was strange to start driving with no real direction, but it was an exciting kind of different. We discerned we should stay in California and headed south to Sacramento.

Oddly enough, our first chance to minister was in the bathroom of a Sacramento mall. We headed into the mall with a backpack full of t-shirts to give away, asking God to show us who needed to hear the gospel or a word of encouragement. As the kids and Matt were waiting in line to use the restroom, the Lord highlighted a woman standing nearby in the hallway. Matt obviously knew nothing about her, but began to ask her how her day was going. As they talked, she shared that she was having a hard time with her special needs son and was going through a lot of emotional distress.

Matt told her that our family was on a mission trip for the Lord and that we wanted to share with her how much Jesus loves her. He explained that Jesus sees her and knows what she's going through, and asked if he and the kids could pray for her. She agreed and they prayed right there in the bathroom hallway. When I came down the hallway looking for them a few minutes later, I saw a woman crying and hugging them. They gave her and her son a shirt as a reminder that God was looking out for them. We took a picture and added her to our prayer list. It was simple, but it was the start of doing ministry together.

We went from city to city, asking God to show us "the one"—that one person who needed Him most in that moment. Sometimes it was a homeless person who needed food and shoes or socks; sometimes it was a person in the grocery store or at the gas station (because RVs cost a lot to fill up!). It was so incredibly refreshing for us and our kids to be reminded that we can be used anywhere, anytime, and with anyone, if we just take time to listen to Jesus.

During a stopover in downtown San Francisco, we walked past a storefront with the sign "Palm Reader." I felt led to go into the store to talk to the palm reader about Jesus. I felt emboldened, yet at the same time, I was nervous. Matt encouraged me to go in and take our daughter Eden with me. She and I waited in the lobby until the female palm reader came to the front. I could sense a spirit of darkness in the building, but decided to remain bold and stay. I asked her what her name was and she told me. She started to ask what type of reading I wanted but I told her I wasn't there for that. I asked her if she knew Jesus. She said, "Yeah, I know Jesus. He speaks to me." I wasn't entirely sure what to do with that information, as I knew that people operating in palm reading and as psychics can also be hearing from the prince of darkness or from his messengers. I told her that I knew Jesus as well and He told me to come in to tell her how much He loves her. She said thank you. I gave her an NHiM hat and a shirt and told her goodbye. I'm not sure what impact that occurrence had on her, but we prayed for her after leaving and I believe it was maybe just a way to be a messenger to speak into her life.

Early on in the trip, we pulled into downtown Santa Cruz to do ministry, but couldn't find a single place to park the RV. We were about to turn around and leave the city when I spotted a space where Matt could parallel park. After pulling over and getting out, we saw the sign on the building we parked in front of. It was an abortion clinic. I started getting concerned, thinking that we may cause offense by the logos on our RV, but Matt felt like it was our opportunity to either pray for or talk to someone going into or coming out of the clinic. We had no intent to protest or show hatred towards anyone at the clinic dealing with a decision that heavy, but it did feel strategic that it was the only parking spot we could find.

We decided to "prayer walk" up and down the street near the clinic, praying for both those faced with tough choices and for the unborn children in the womb. Interestingly enough, we never saw anyone enter or leave the building during that hour or so. We decided to take a longer prayer walk around the city. Maybe even just parking the RV there that afternoon may have reminded someone of God's hand upon their life. It could have possibly even deterred someone from making a choice they would someday regret. Regardless, we took it as an afternoon to just pray over the city, because sometimes prayer is the greatest need of all.

We ended up spending almost half our time in Los Angeles, unplanned of course. We began ministering to families in the RV park, strangers on the streets or on the beach—wherever we sensed His direction to go. We'd heard of a ministry called the Dream Center in the heart of LA. We called them to see if they needed any help that week, and they did. We discovered so much about this incredible ministry that was birthed from the heart of one man and his wife. It

TAKING IT TO THE STREETS

is a very robust ministry, resulting from the "yes" of one couple. We partnered for quite a few days with the Dream Center. Together with our kids, we were able to cook and serve food in their kitchen, which feeds thousands of people for free each day. We went to 'skid row' to pass out 100 pairs of flip flops that we purchased to donate to the homeless, along with hot food and sanitization packs for those living on the streets. It was a very sobering experience for us and our kids to see how people lived on these dangerous city blocks of L.A.

We also did a block party with the Dream Center in a park where many homeless lived. This is a memory we hold dear to our hearts. We had a bunch of shirts and water bottles, granola bars, socks, flip flops, and more to give out to everyone in need that we met. In the process, we met an older gentleman named Frank who was homeless. He said he was a veteran and was injured in war, which made him in permanent need of a wheelchair. We asked him if we could pray for his legs and he said yes. As he sat in his wheelchair, our kids and Matt prayed over him for healing. He smiled graciously and hugged us. Then he *stood up* and got out of his wheelchair and started to walk! He kept walking, pushing his own wheelchair down the sidewalk! We couldn't believe it. He said his legs felt so much better and the pain was almost gone, and he wanted to walk. We thanked God! We left in awe of God's faithfulness to answer simple prayers prayed in full faith.

Of course, we know that God doesn't always answer prayers in the way we hope for and that we don't always receive the outcome we desire. We also understand that bad things can happen to good people. We don't have all the answers and don't believe that you are lacking faith if your prayer isn't answered in the time or in the way you expected, but we also know that God is sovereign and loves all His children. We can't always explain why certain things happen the way they do, but God still wants relationship and communion with us and asks us to trust Him in all things.

If you've experienced unanswered prayers or trials, we sympathize with you and pray that God brings you peace, protection, comfort, provision, or a breakthrough. "Rejoice always, pray continually, give thanks in all circumstances; for this is God's will for you in Christ Jesus." (1 Thessalonians 5:16-18)

We experienced many other beautiful 'God-moments' and miracles during our family mission trip. We watched our kids blossom, developing greater spiritual maturity and discernment. They displayed great love in simple ways to so many. We gifted our kids with new Bibles before the trip and we all spent more focused time reading the word of God during our travels. We practiced hearing God through His word and through prayer. The RV was like the "NHiM gospel truck," spreading the hope and love of Jesus. It was a beautiful thing.

TAKING IT TO THE STREETS

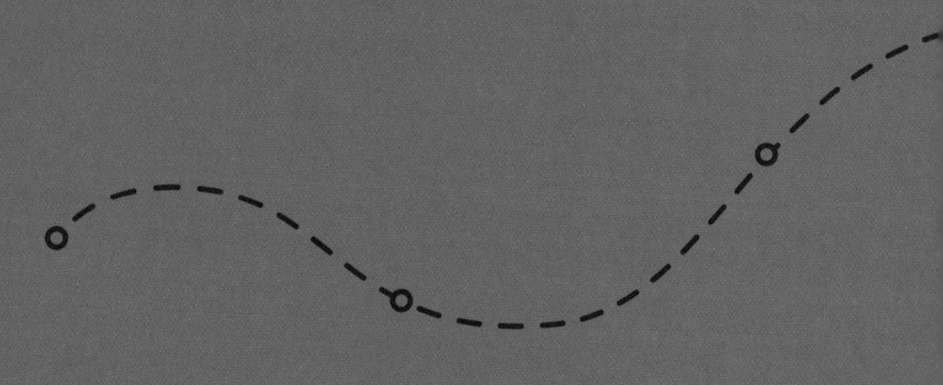

Part Five

CRUISING ALTITUDE

Have you ever felt a gentle whisper of an idea that seems too crazy to pursue? A feeling to do something out of your comfort zone, or an urge to choose a path that seems impossible? Could God be prompting you with an idea? How do you know? John 10:27 says, "My sheep listen to my voice; I know them, and they follow me." And in Isaiah 55:8-9, the Lord says: "My thoughts are nothing like your thoughts…My ways are far beyond anything you could imagine. For just as the heavens are higher than the earth, so my ways are higher than your ways and my thoughts higher than your thoughts."

You see, to hear God's voice, you must be in relationship with Him. And relationship with Him begins with conversation. Healthy conversations are two-sided — there's both talking and listening. But what if you don't hear God's voice in response? Listening takes practice. Psalm 119:15 says to study God's word and meditate on it, which means "to think deeply or focus one's mind for a period of time, in silence." It's not a quick-fix method. God's word is our love letter from Him. And meditating on it while engaging in conversation with Him is the secret recipe to a healthy and vibrant relationship.

So I ask you, how's your conversation with Jesus? Are you in God's word? Is it consistent and regular or only when you have an emergency? I urge you to take time to invest in the greatest relationship you'll ever have. Read His love letter. Talk to Him. LISTEN to him. Pause in His presence. Then, follow with great faith. Everything else in life can wait.

– Matt

Chapter 21

HAWAIIAN STATE OF MIND

"Aloha is the spirit of God at work in you and in me and in the world, uniting what is separated, overcoming darkness and death, bringing new light and life to all who sit in the darkness of fear, guiding the feet of humankind into the way of peace."

—*Rev. Dr. Abraham Akaka*

SEVERE TURBULENCE

In December 2022, our good friends gave us a week and a half to stay in their timeshare in Kauai for free. Overworked from the Christmas season, we desperately needed a vacation and couldn't pass it up. We'd been producing clothing non-stop for months, plus shipping 500 or more orders a day. By that point, the brand had grown to over $1.2 million in sales, doubling in one year's time. It could only have been God.

Grateful for the incredible gift from our friends, we found affordable plane tickets and headed to the breathtaking island of Kauai. It was like nothing we'd seen before—lush and green, with gorgeous turquoise waters and the stately NaPali Coast. Matt and I fell in love. We all did! So much so, that our daughters cried on the flight back home because they didn't want to leave!

While in Kauai, the Lord whispered to our heart to pause and rest. We'd been so busy with the day-to-day endless tasks of printing and fulfillment that we could no longer stop long enough to think or dream about the next five to 10 years ahead of us. The entire heart behind NHiM was to pursue ministry over business, and something needed to shift.

A few months earlier, Matt had experienced a vivid dream in which he was a fighter pilot in an old bomber plane—kind of like one out of World War I. He was in the fight of his life, piloting his plane, shooting and defending himself against the enemy in war, all while trying to just stay alive. The scenery around him was dark and gloomy, full of wartime terrors and labor. Then out of nowhere, the stressful scene transformed. The war was over and he was transported to a pleasant place. He was handed the keys to a commercial plane and presented with all the benefits and perks that came along with the job. His flying days would be smooth, with very little to no stress, and he'd be able to put the plane on autopilot for the duration of most flights. Instead of feeling relieved, Matt was perplexed. It seemed so easy, it almost felt wrong.

Matt had awoken from the dream and known it was from the Lord. But it wasn't until our trip to Kauai that he understood what it meant.

During our vacation, God began to show us new ways to operate NHiM so we wouldn't have to spend all our time in the hustle. He revealed to us new ministries that lay deep within our hearts to pursue. We wanted to gather people around a table to have genuine fellowship, with discipleship at its core. We wanted to start a house of worship and prayer, impact the youth and young adults, continue spreading the gospel and doing missions. We wanted to author multiple books and champion people to fall madly in love with Jesus—to pursue God at all costs.

I know it sounds silly to say you're called to Hawaii (sure....) but there was an invitation to follow Him. It was crazy to think of uprooting our lives again and moving our family to the middle of the Pacific ocean, but we felt the time had come to move toward the next phase of the mission. Now we needed to pray and see if Jesus was in this or not.

We went back home and had a serious conversation about what it would take to make the move happen. It could be our chance to eradicate some of those large, high-interest debts from the store buildouts. The only way to do that was to sell our home and absolutely everything in it. We'd need to find new homes for our sweet farm animals. We'd also need to sell the screen printing business and find a new source for NHiM's production, warehousing, and fulfillment.

It seemed impossible. How could we do it all? Like a bird trapped in a cage, we didn't know how to get out. A month later, Matt and I took a second trip to Kauai to pray about it, see if we could find a home to rent, and explore the potential of making it work. While on the trip, one of our garment suppliers connected us to a full-service fulfillment company based out of Los Angeles. The timing was surreal. We jumped on a call to connect with their team and talk about the potential of working together. It felt good. We looked over quotes and were told we could transfer everything over to them in as soon as two months. It seemed too good to be true.

Next up was our home. We had to interview realtors, get it on the market, and pray it would sell for what we needed it to in order to pay off our debts. We were asking a lot in a buyer's market. Interest rates were climbing and homes in the area were not selling fast. The odds were not in our favor. We hoped to be moved in the coming summer, before school started up again for our kids. We listed the home and everything in it as a package deal. It was time to sell it all—every plate and dish, every piece of furniture we'd collected over almost 20 years of marriage, all except one suitcase each. Our few boxes of keepsakes would be shipped off to Matt's parents' house for safekeeping during the transition.

Then there was the business and the staff. We had several employees running the printing and fulfillment. Our creative director, marketer, and customer care manager worked remotely, so the move wouldn't impact them. But we still had a few months left on the warehouse lease and a ton of equipment and materials. It seemed unrealistic to think we could sell it all and move in time.

Our house had several showings and we talked to a potential buyer for our business, but nothing solidified. One weekend, while our house was being rented out through Airbnb, we were staying at our friend's house and heard a powerful sermon about waiting on God. The gist of the message was that sometimes God is waiting for you to act in faith before you see His provision—rather than waiting on His provision in order to act. Sometimes we have a "beggar's mentality" when we come to God in prayer, when in reality He's already empowered us with the faith to move mountains. We just need to make them move.

Matt and I felt like the Lord was speaking to us. I told Matt, "I think we're just supposed to book one-way tickets to Kauai. Worst case, we cancel our flights and lose the money." We found cheap (really cheap) one-way tickets for June 22, 2023 and booked them for our family. And then we prayed, asking God to honor our faith by moving everything into place to allow this transition to happen.

Literally a week later, on June 7, we got an offer on our house, animals, and belongings, and we sold our business and cars. Can you believe that?? God is so good!! And seven is God's number—it signifies completion and perfection. God rested on the seventh day, and we sensed that the Lord was bringing us into a season of rest. The fact that it all happened on the seventh felt like a hug from God.

With one suitcase each and my two guitars, we flew from SFO to Kauai to stay in our new rental home on the North Shore. Everything was set for NHiM to operate without us being physically present. All the clothing was being produced and fulfilled by our new supplier in Los Angeles. A small dream team of talented, Jesus-loving individuals ran the creative, marketing, and customer experience departments. We planned to have weekly video meetings with our team to connect, inspire, and give direction to the overall vision for where the brand was heading. Our girls were accepted to attend a small Christian school on the island with wonderful teachers and students. The beach was a five-minute drive away. Only Jesus could do this.

Matt's dream had symbolized what we'd been doing the last nine years. We'd been in the fight of our lives for almost a decade, pursuing our purpose. We'd been in non-stop severe turbulence, trying to keep the business above ground, and to avoid plummeting into financial disaster. Many times it was scary. We were doing all we could to keep on the "flight path" and not lose heart. Little did we know, we were about to step into the next phase of flying. God was going to give us the keys to a smoother flight. Things would become easier. We wouldn't have to run at full speed anymore.

***

Now, here we are, living the life we could've only dreamed of. We have entered a Hawaiian state of mind. There's a reason why Aloha is the greeting and goodbye used by locals. The definition of "aloha" embodies peace, grace, affection, compassion, respect, the full context of love, and much more. Moving to Hawaii was not just about a beautiful destination, but rather a step to renew the spirit and acquire a new mindset.

Our kids and family are thriving. The small island of Kauai feels reminiscent of what the Garden of Eden must've looked like. We've hosted prayer and worship nights and begun a cooking/discipleship group for teens. We are serving the community in different ways, including gathering people around the table as the center of fellowship, and working to create a sustainable ministry with other like-minded leaders. We are praying carefully about each thing we put our hand to in ministry. We have big vision and many dreams for what's next, but we'll only act on them if God opens the door. But the beautiful thing is, we don't feel stressed or overworked – we feel the physical "selah" mentioned in the book of Psalms. We are learning to rest in God and find peace just being in His presence.

Matt has always said that NHiM Apparel was the vehicle to take us to our destination. So what's to come? In the famous words of Dr. Emmett Brown (in *Back to the Future*—Matt's favorite movie of all time):

"Roads? Where we're going, we don't need roads."

Besides, we're still mid-flight. Only God knows what lies ahead for NHiM.

HAWAIIAN STATE OF MIND

 **Chapter 22**

NUMBERS DON'T LIE

"If you have anything, or if I have anything, it's because it's been given to us by our Creator."

—David Green, founder of Hobby Lobby

SEVERE TURBULENCE

When this book hits the shelves, it will have been 10 years since the dream of NHiM began. We have carried this dream fervently and faithfully since its birth, nurturing it from infancy through childhood, providing for its every need. The many times it was on life support, we never gave up or pulled the plug, instead praying for a miracle each time and seeing God always come through. In the process, we've witnessed more blessings and miracles than one could hope for in a lifetime. No matter where God may lead us or the NHiM brand, the pursuit of our purpose in Christ and the existence of the brand is all for the glory of God.

Achievements:

- Became a multi-million dollar brand
- Worn in over 53 countries across the globe
- Prayed with: an estimated 250,000+ people (either in person, online, at events, through our prayer hotline, and through prayer cards sent)
- Thousands of testimonies or answered prayers, including healings
- Gave away countless free Bibles
- Opened an orphanage for 12 children in Telangana, India

None of these achievements compare to the glory or goodness of God; nonetheless, it has amazed us to step back and see all that has been accomplished in this journey so far, and the small part we've played in facilitating the dream of NHiM in our lives. It hasn't been easy, but the prayer stats alone has made it all worthwhile.

This is not a story about the triumphs or monetary success of NHiM. This is a story about faith and purpose. We are nothing on our own, without the righteousness of Jesus. We have chosen to fully fall in love with Jesus, surrender our hearts to His vision for our lives, and trust God above every voice around us. To dream with God and to ask Him why He created us. We're not satisfied with a mediocre life. We want to live life in the abundance of who God called us to be, never settling on "good enough." There's no mistake, we haven't arrived or reached perfection, and we won't until we reach Heaven.

Let's talk about you for a minute. If you were handed a plane ticket today to the destination of your dreams, with just one catch — that to get to your destination you would experience the most severe turbulence you've ever faced with no guarantee of survival, but with the opportunity of a life fulfilled with no regrets — would you take the ticket? It's a tough question. Discovering your God-given purpose and going after it is a lot like this scenario. The journey to pursue Jesus and fulfill your purpose is often accompanied by severe turbulence. The choice for a mediocre life or a fulfilled life *NHiM* is yours to make.

So…why were you created? And what are you doing today to go after all that God has for you? Don't live an unfulfilled life. Be willing to risk everything, even if it means going through severe turbulence, in order to arrive at the destination God has chosen for you. "Have I not commanded you? Be strong and courageous. Do not be afraid; do not be discouraged, for the Lord your God will be with you wherever you go." (Joshua 1:9)

Your flight is now boarding.

OUR PRAYER FOR YOU

We pray that fear would not grip you,
but God's unconditional love would surround you.

We pray that anxiety would not overtake you,
but His perfect peace would define you.

We pray that sin would not hold you prisoner,
but the Spirit of life would give you full freedom.

We pray that no sickness or affliction would be on you,
but only health and wholeness in Him would remain.

We pray that no weapon or plans formed against you would prevail,
but only God's best for you would prosper.

We pray every need would be met, all heaviness be lifted, all wisdom
be given, and that His presence go before you.

May you be marked today by our Creator,
to know the great significance He holds for your life,
and to know how deeply loved you are.

Amen.

THROUGH THE YEARS...

NHiM Kiosk opened in Park Meadows Mall, 2015

Heavenfest in Colorado, 2015

Inside the first NHiM store, 2016

Stepping off the bus to meet the kids in Ibrahimpatnam, India, 2016

Cutting the ribbon on our orphanage in India, 2016

NHiM Orphanage, 2016

Hugging our orphanage "house mom"

Sneaking a kiss in India

Giving gifts to the children at the grand opening of the orphanage, 2016

Lajes Field in Terceria, emergency landing after severe turbulence, 2016

First NHiM Store, November 2016

Leaving Park Meadows Mall to head out on the National Tour, summer of 2016

NHiM Store remodel completed, 2017

Diane leading worship

Family photo in Redding, CA, 2018

Pop-Up Store in Redding, CA, 2018

Screen printing on an automatic press at the NHiM warehouse, 2020

Matt & Diane, NHiM product shoot, 2020

NHiM Warehouse in Redding, CA, 2021

Matt, aka "the Goat Father"

Family photo with goats, "Kardashian style," 2021

Surfing outreach ministry, Pismo Beach, CA, 2021

NHiM e-bike giveaway, 2020

NHiM Warehouse in Redding, CA

NHiM RV, Family Mission Trip, 2022

Family photo, 2023

"Moving to Kauai day," June 2023

Matt & Diane in Kauai, Hawaii

ACKNOWLEDGEMENTS

ACKNOWLEDGMENTS

There have been so many incredible people who have come alongside us in the journey. Thank you, thank you, thank you. NHiM would not be here were it not for each of you who believed in the message of the brand enough to wear it on your sleeve. This story has come to life through each of your lives.

To Mike Heath. Thank you for helping us in the very beginning to bring the dream to life through your insane gifting. Your talent and drive is inspirational to us.

To our parents, Doug & Margie and Ken & Cheryl. Thank you for all the prayers in the midnight hours, the support when we needed it, and for allowing us to lean on you for wisdom. Your faith, kindness, and love for Jesus is inspiring.

To Cammy, for managing the NHiM store so well and raising up an on-fire, Jesus-loving staff!

To Ken, for the business guidance, wisdom, and analytics over the years.

To our extended family. We love each and every one of you! Thank you for wearing the first NHiM shirts, sharing with so many of your friends, and encouraging our steps to get us to today.

To our dear friend, Jamie Klusacek. What can we say? You are a pure gift! Thank you for the countless memories worshiping the King of Kings together and for all the laughter. It's been a joy watching our kids grow up together, even though they are now miles apart. You have always championed running further with Jesus and reaching every goal within our hearts. We love you, dear friend!

To Milan, thank you for the years of friendship, family vacations, and double-dates together, and for your gift of making the pages of this book come alive through incredible visual design.

To our editor, Suzanne. Your gift with the written word is unmatched. You are such a joy to work with and you truly brought our words and book to the next level, so thank you. May our combined efforts impact countless lives.

To our first employee, Cassandra Green. Thank you for stepping out and taking a risk on us. Thank you for loving customers so well.

Your enthusiasm for the brand spread like wildfire!

To all the original team members: Nancy Garcia, for your love of ministry and your talent behind the lens and in design; to evangelists Neil Sanderlin and Ruvim Yaremkiv for leaving a good paying job, moving all the way from Alaska, and always listening to the Holy Spirit for each customer who walked in; to Ryan Tims, for a friendship that means more than you know, for your prophetic insights, for the conversation at the Southwest Plaza kiosk that one afternoon, and for being a part of NHiM from the very beginning through now. Thanks for becoming an absolute wizard at marketing!!

To our nephew, Levi, for shooting cool NHiM commercials and epic lifestyle shoots. Your joy and friendship has always blessed us!

To Angel House founders, Lindsay & Dominic Russo. Thank you for stewarding a vision from the Lord to help so many children in India find forever homes.

To Pastors John & Chris Leach and Jubilee Fellowship Church, for the early support of the brand.

To our Creative Director extraordinaire, Matthew Warren. Your unique perspective on art and faith invites everyone to the table of NHiM. Thank you for sharing your many gifts and making NHiM what it is today.

To our staff who have taken care of our online customers so well, from Aubrey, to Amy, to Becca, to Bella. Your care and prayers have impacted so many!!

To the two families we did life, ministry, and work with—Matt and Aubrey, and CP and Amy. The memories and moments are a priceless gift!

To Brita and John Fay, for your friendship and mentorship. You are lifelong friends to us.

To Jake & Hannah Ouellette and Thrive Church for your support in the early years.

To Park Meadows Mall, for believing in our vision!

To Jesus Sandoval, for showing up to help us install floors, and to teaching us all about screen printing! Thank you for your friendship.

ACKNOWLEDGMENTS

To Tim and Nicol, for your friendship and generosity in hosting us in your mom's home on Kauai!

To the Bethel Church Leadership, including Joel Power (and your word to us in 2018), Sarah Cooper and the Bethel Online Campus, Toni Matta, and the Bethel Media family.

To Gabe Cooper & the CCV Family for your partnership and for carrying our merch in your church!

To surfing goat extraordinaire and friend, Dana McGregor. Yiiiieeee!

To Grace & Lace owners, Melissa & Rick Hinnant, for your mentorship at the get-go.

To Shantel, for sewing thousands of tags on our garments!!

To Don & Evan Hanson, for believing in us and helping us turn a kiosk into a storefront.

To our architect, Emily of Neoera, for creating such a unique, stunning, aesthetic look for the NHiM store.

To Sophia Motsinger, for modeling so many clothes!

To the anonymous donor who gifted us the money in the mail, thank you for your generosity.

To our beautiful daughters. Bella, you inspire us with your zeal for the Lord! Keep singing and shining for Jesus. Jewel, thank you for your deep questions about the Bible, your intense love for the Lord, and your authentic worship. Eden, thank you for being our third gift! You bring us joy, you are talented in sports, music and school, and you help us make it to places on time! We love you all so much—what a gift you are to us.

We hope we've acknowledged each and every one of you, yet I know there's countless more—too many to list.

Above all, to the King of Kings, for entrusting us to carry this message into the world. May we catch a glimpse of your face more clearly, every day.

From Diane

To my husband and best friend, Matt. You make me a better version of me just by being around you. 20 years together have flown by! I love everything about you—your charisma, the testimonies you share with strangers, the inspiration you carry to everyone you meet, the joy you have in the Lord, the way you lead our family so well, and the vision you carry out so well (oh, and your good looks!). Let's keep living life to the fullest and lighting up the darkness! I love you!! Here's to all the years to come!

From Matt

And last but certainly not least, to the voice and words behind a vast majority of this book; my unmatched, unrivaled, beautiful beyond compare, the G.O.A.T., my one and only, the greatest gift from God, my best friend, my co-pilot, my Batwoman and my better half. I love you. I love our journey. I love your faith. Thank you for believing in me. Thank you for saying yes to blind pursuits. Thank you for sacrificing. Thank you for leading. Thank you for loving. Thank you for our precious girls. Excited for the journeys ahead. Excited for the testimonies to come. May Jesus always be the wind behind our sail. This book is a testimony of our past but a launchpad for both us and the reader into a prophetic future of continued faith. May it bless and appoint each reader, our kids, our kids' kids, and generations to come. We love you all.

ABOUT THE AUTHORS

Diane and Matt Allen, husband and wife, are the passionate, resilient business creators behind the NHiM Apparel brand. They are devoted to living life fully for Jesus and sharing that joy with others. Originally from Colorado, they now reside on the beautiful island of Kauai with their three stunning daughters.

Diane is a worship leader, writer, and community builder who thrives on leading others into authentic encounters with Jesus. When she's not writing or leading worship, she loves to cook tasty, plant-based food, have impromptu dance parties with her family, and drink good coffee with dear friends.

Matt holds a bachelor's degree in finance and has a proven track record of helping start-ups take off. He is a visionary leader with a heart for coaching others to reach their highest potential, both in business and in Christ. His gift for brand building is matched by his passion for helping others succeed in their God-given purpose. His love for animals is only rivaled by his enthusiasm for college football and great food.

Together, Diane and Matt are committed to building community and inspiring others to live wholeheartedly for Jesus.

CONNECT WITH US

Instagram
@NHIMAPPAREL
@IAMDIANEALLEN
@MATTHEWDUANEALLEN

TikTok
@nhimapparel.com

THREADS
@nhimapparel

Visit us Online
www.nhimapparel.com

Contact Us
info@nhimapparel.com

Invite Matt & Diane to speak at your church, event, or podcast
admin@nhimapparel.com